Euthanasia
Opposing Viewpoints®

Other Books of Related Interest in the Opposing Viewpoints Series:

Euthanasia
Opposing Viewpoints®

David Bender & Bruno Leone, *Series Editors*

Carol Wekesser, *Book Editor*

OPPOSING
VIEWPOINTS
SERIES®

Greenhaven Press, Inc., San Diego, CA

Greenhaven Press, Inc.
PO Box 289009
San Diego, CA 92198-9009

Cover photo: Rocky Theis

Library of Congress Cataloging-in-Publication Data

Euthanasia : opposing viewpoints / Carol Wekesser, book editor.
    p.   cm. — (Opposing viewpoints series)
  Includes bibliographical references and index.
  ISBN 1-56510-244-4 (lib. bdg. : acid-free paper) —
ISBN 1-56510-243-6 (pbk. : acid-free paper)
  1. Euthanasia [1. Euthanasia.] I. Wekesser, Carol, 1963–
II. Series: Opposing viewpoints series (Unnumbered)
R726.E7924   1995
179'.7—dc20   94-41046
                                              CIP0
                                                AC

"Congress shall make no law . . .
abridging the freedom of speech,
or of the press."

First Amendment to the U.S. Constitution

The basic foundation of our democracy is the First Amendment
guarantee of freedom of expression. The Opposing Viewpoints
Series is dedicated to the concept of this basic freedom and the
idea that it is more important to practice it than to enshrine it.

Contents

Why Consider Opposing Viewpoints?

"The only way in which a human being can make some approach to knowing the whole of a subject is by hearing what can be said about it by persons of every variety of opinion and studying all modes in which it can be looked at by every character of mind. No wise man ever acquired his wisdom in any mode but this."

John Stuart Mill

In our media-intensive culture it is not difficult to find differing opinions. Thousands of newspapers and magazines and dozens of radio and television talk shows resound with differing points of view. The difficulty lies in deciding which opinion to agree with and which "experts" seem the most credible. The more inundated we become with differing opinions and claims, the more essential it is to hone critical reading and thinking skills to evaluate these ideas. Opposing Viewpoints books address this problem directly by presenting stimulating debates that can be used to enhance and teach these skills. The varied opinions contained in each book examine many different aspects of a single issue. While examining these conveniently edited opposing views, readers can develop critical thinking skills such as the ability to compare and contrast authors' credibility, facts, argumentation styles, use of persuasive techniques, and other stylistic tools. In short, the Opposing Viewpoints Series is an ideal way to attain the higher-level thinking and reading skills so essential in a culture of diverse and contradictory opinions.

In addition to providing a tool for critical thinking, Opposing Viewpoints books challenge readers to question their own strongly held opinions and assumptions. Most people form their opinions on the basis of upbringing, peer pressure, and personal, cultural, or professional bias. By reading carefully balanced opposing views, readers must directly confront new ideas as well as the opinions of those with whom they disagree. This is not to simplistically argue that everyone who reads opposing views will—or should—change his or her opinion. Instead, the series enhances readers' depth of understanding of their own views by encouraging confrontation with opposing ideas. Careful examination of others' views can lead to the readers' understanding of the logical inconsistencies in their own opinions, perspective on why they hold an opinion, and the consideration of the possibility that their opinion requires further evaluation.

Evaluating Other Opinions

To ensure that this type of examination occurs, Opposing Viewpoints books present all types of opinions. Prominent spokespeople on different sides of each issue as well as well-known professionals from many disciplines challenge the reader. An additional goal of the series is to provide a forum for other, less known, or even unpopular viewpoints. The opinion of an ordinary person who has had to make the decision to cut off life support from a terminally ill relative, for example, may be just as valuable and provide just as much insight as a medical ethicist's professional opinion. The editors have two additional purposes in including these less known views. One, the editors encourage readers to respect others' opinions—even when not enhanced by professional credibility. It is only by reading or listening to and objectively evaluating others' ideas that one can determine whether they are worthy of consideration. Two, the inclusion of such viewpoints encourages the important critical thinking skill of objectively evaluating an author's credentials and bias. This evaluation will illuminate an author's reasons for taking a particular stance on an issue and will aid in readers' evaluation of the author's ideas.

As series editors of the Opposing Viewpoints Series, it is our hope that these books will give readers a deeper understanding of the issues debated and an appreciation of the complexity of even seemingly simple issues when good and honest people disagree. This awareness is particularly important in a democratic society such as ours in which people enter into public debate to determine the common good. Those with whom one disagrees should not be regarded as enemies but rather as people whose views deserve careful examination and may shed light on one's own.

Thomas Jefferson once said that "difference of opinion leads to inquiry, and inquiry to truth." Jefferson, a broadly educated man, argued that "if a nation expects to be ignorant and free . . . it expects what never was and never will be." As individuals and as a nation, it is imperative that we consider the opinions of others and examine them with skill and discernment. The Opposing Viewpoints Series is intended to help readers achieve this goal.

David L. Bender & Bruno Leone,
Series Editors

Introduction

"I do not believe that any man fears to be dead, but only the stroke of death."

Francis Bacon (1561-1626)

In recent decades, medical advances have allowed physicians to prolong life to a greater extent than ever before. While this on the surface may appear to be a positive development, many people now fear living too long in ways they would not choose: dependent upon machines, unconscious, or in terrible pain. To address their fears, many people are attempting to control how and when they die. This movement has fostered debate concerning euthanasia.

Merriam-Webster's Collegiate Dictionary: Tenth Edition defines euthanasia as "the act or practice of killing or permitting the death of hopelessly sick or injured individuals . . . in a relatively painless way for reasons of mercy." But the euthanasia debate encompasses far more than this definition may indicate. Understanding the various forms of euthanasia is important if one is to grasp the complexities of the issue and why it inspires such emotion.

When people refer to "euthanasia," they may be discussing passive euthanasia, active euthanasia, and/or assisted suicide. Passive euthanasia occurs when medical treatment for a serious illness or injury is stopped and the patient is allowed to die. The most common act of passive euthanasia is the removal of a respirator on which a dying patient is dependent. Physicians or family members decide to disconnect the respirator so that the patient dies sooner—and perhaps with less suffering—than he or she would have with the respirator.

In active euthanasia, someone—perhaps a physician or family member—takes the life of a patient before he or she dies of a terminal illness or injury. For example, it is active euthanasia when a family member gives a dying patient a lethal injection. The patient dies from the injection, not from the disease or injury.

Finally, assisted suicide occurs when someone—usually a physician, family member, or friend—fulfills a person's request for help in dying. This usually involves a terminally ill patient who wishes to die, but cannot complete the act alone—he or she may need a physician to give a lethal prescription or a family member to help arrange some other means of suicide. In the case of assisted suicide, the patient, while receiving help, alone performs the final, death-inducing act.

To dedicated supporters or opponents of active euthanasia, passive euthanasia, and assisted suicide, the distinctions among the three may be unimportant. Fierce defenders of the right to life, for example, may view all three types of action as immoral and may consequently use the term "euthanasia" when discussing any action that hastens death. People who strongly support the right to die—that is, the right of an individual to choose when and how death will occur—also may not make a distinction among active and passive euthanasia and assisted suicide.

However, these distinctions are important to many in the debate. For example, Professors Robert Campbell and Diane Collinson argue that while passive euthanasia is ethical and acceptable, active euthanasia is not. The distinction between active and passive euthanasia, they believe, "is crucial, marking out the ethical boundary between recognizing that human life is finite and acting as executioner." The late sociologist William McCord also supported passive euthanasia but opposed active euthanasia. He supported assisted suicide, calling it "the final proof of man's independence and self-control; an affirmation of man's ultimate liberty."

Some of the most noted court cases concerning euthanasia illustrate the importance of the distinctions among active euthanasia, passive euthanasia, and assisted suicide. The case of Karen Ann Quinlan is perhaps the most famous because it was the first to bring the issue of euthanasia to public attention. Quinlan lapsed into an irreversible coma in 1975 after consuming alcohol and tranquilizers at a party. Her parents asked that she be removed from a respirator. In a landmark 1976 case, the New Jersey Supreme Court agreed and allowed the Quinlans to have the respirator disconnected.

Although Quinlan breathed on her own and lived for another nine years after being removed from the respirator, her case was the first instance of a court's approving passive euthanasia as a legal action. At the time of the Quinlan case, no one was suggesting that active euthanasia or assisted suicide should be considered for legalization; the distinction between passive and active euthanasia was important to the court and the public at that time.

In the 1980s, the fine line between active and passive euthanasia came to the public's attention in the case of Nancy Cruzan. When Cruzan was left in an irreversible coma after a 1983 car accident, her parents asked that the machine keeping her alive be removed. Unlike the Quinlan case, however, Cruzan was not on a respirator; the "machine" keeping her alive was a feeding tube that provided her with hydration and nutrition. After many years in court, in 1990 the Cruzans finally were allowed to have her feeding tube removed, after which she died.

The Cruzans believed that removing the feeding tube was passive euthanasia: to them, the tube was a medical treatment keeping their daughter alive. To those who opposed their actions, however, the Cruzans had intentionally killed their daughter through starvation. Even Joseph Quinlan, Karen Ann's father, responded with astonishment when asked in 1976 if he would seek to have his daughter's feeding tube removed: "Oh, no," he responded, "that is her nourishment." Many Americans in the 1970s would have agreed with Quinlan, viewing passive euthanasia as ethical but opposing most cases of active euthanasia or assisted suicide. The fact that the Cruzans received much public support shows how public opinion had changed in just over a decade. More people began to argue that measures such as those taken by the Cruzans could sometimes be acceptable and should be legal.

By the 1990s, the person most responsible for focusing public attention on the issues of euthanasia and assisted suicide was retired pathologist Jack Kevorkian. Between 1990 and November 1994, Kevorkian assisted in the suicides of twenty-one terminally or severely chronically ill patients. Kevorkian has garnered both vehement opposition and strong support. For example, publisher Malcolm S. Forbes Jr. calls Kevorkian a "serial killer," while writer Betty Rollin calls him a "fearless reformer." Many Americans consider Kevorkian's actions extreme and immoral. But many support what he advocates: the right to die.

A 1993 national public opinion poll indicated that 73 percent of Americans support physician-assisted suicide. Why are Americans, who only two decades ago were sharply divided on the passive euthanasia in the Quinlan case, increasingly in support of euthanasia and assisted suicide? Perhaps the increased cost of health care has brought out the practicality in Americans, who see no point in bankrupting their families just so that they themselves can live for a few more weeks or months. Or perhaps it is because people fear the kind of death medical technology too often seems to offer: long, drawn-out suffering from cancer or other painful illness. As Wiley Morrison, president of the Kansas City chapter of the Hemlock Society, states: "Forty or fifty years ago, you would go quickly and painlessly. Now they've cured us of infectious diseases, but we end up getting cancer. Cancer can be horribly painful. Death is preferred to that kind of life for some people."

Whatever the reason, Americans are worried about how they will die, and the debate concerning euthanasia and assisted suicide has become a national issue. *Euthanasia: Opposing Viewpoints* examines this debate in the following chapters: Is Euthanasia Ethical? Should Euthanasia Be Legalized? Should Physicians Assist in Euthanasia? Who Should Make Decisions About Euthanasia? Is Infant Euthanasia Ethical? The contributors to these chapters shed light on the complex ethical and legal issues involved in the national discussion on euthanasia.

Is Euthanasia Ethical?

Euthanasia

Chapter Preface

To determine whether any action is ethical, a society looks to its values and to those elements—whether religious teachings, the writings of philosophers, the teachings of great leaders, or spoken traditions—that help determine these values. This is also true in the controversy over euthanasia. As Americans attempt to determine whether euthanasia is ever ethical and, if so, in what circumstances, many look especially to their religious teachings for guidance.

Interpretations of the Bible and other religious books vary, leaving people to disagree on the ethicality of euthanasia. Some Christians, Jews, and followers of other faiths strongly oppose euthanasia, believing it to be against the will of God. As hospice director Ronald Otremba states, "God is the sole creator of life and has sovereign authority over life and death. To some, this principle may seem cruel and unsympathetic, but it is, on the contrary, very respectful of the individual's needs and dignity. No matter what the condition of a person's life, there is still value in it."

In contrast, there are numerous religious Americans who believe that the compassion and mercy taught by Christ and others can be shown through euthanasia. In addition, they argue that God has given humans free will, including the will to choose their own time of death. As Chicago rabbi Joseph Edelheit states, "There is a strong indication that scripture allows us this final act of free will. Even if some choose to interpret the final act of dying to belong only to the divine giver of life, the human has control until it is wrested from him or her."

Euthanasia is so controversial that even Americans with a common faith have trouble finding common ground on the issue. In the following chapter, the contributors explore the ethics of euthanasia, using religion, philosophy, and other disciplines to present their debates.

"A caring society . . . offers euthanasia to hopelessly sick persons as an act of love."

Euthanasia Is Ethical

Derek Humphry

Derek Humphry founded the Hemlock Society in 1980 and was its executive director until 1992. Today he is president of the Euthanasia Research and Guidance Organization. The address of ERGO is: 24829 Norris Lane, Junction City, OR 97448. Phone/fax 503-998-1873. E-mail: dhumphry@efn.org. Humphry is the author of several books on euthanasia, including *Jean's Way, Final Exit,* and *Dying with Dignity,* from which the following viewpoint is excerpted. In the viewpoint, Humphry describes two forms of suicide: suicide for mental health reasons, which both he and the Hemlock Society oppose; and justifiable suicide, or "autoeuthanasia." He argues that autoeuthanasia is an acceptable choice for those suffering from terminal illness or severe physical handicap, and he outlines the conditions under which it can be considered an ethical act.

As you read, consider the following questions:

1. According to Humphry, what is the Greek root of the word *euthanasia?*
2. How does the author respond to the argument that suffering is ennobling?
3. How does the knowledge that euthanasia is an option for them affect some patients, according to Humphry?

From DYING WITH DIGNITY: *Understanding Euthanasia* by Derek Humphry. Copyright © 1992 by Derek Humphry. Published by arrangement with Carol Publishing Group. A Birch Lane Press Book.

The Hemlock Society is dedicated to the view that there are at least two forms of suicide. One is emotional suicide, or irrational self murder in all its complexities. Let me emphasize that the Hemlock Society view on that form of suicide is approximately the same as the American Association of Suicidology, and the rest of society, which is to prevent it where you can. We do not encourage any form of suicide for mental health or unhappy reasons.

But we say that there is a second form of suicide: justifiable suicide. That is, rational and planned self-deliverance. Put another way, this is autoeuthanasia, using suicide as the means. I don't think the word "suicide" really sits well in this context, but we are stuck with it. . . .

The word "euthanasia" comes from the Greek—*eu*, good and *thanatos*, death. But there has been a more complex meaning developed in recent times. The word euthanasia has now come to mean doing something about achieving a good death. Doing something, either positive or negative, about getting that good death.

When Is Suicide Ethical?

Suicide can be justified ethically by the average Hemlock Society supporter for the following reasons:

One. Advanced terminal illness which is causing unbearable suffering to that individual. This is the most common reason for self-deliverance.

Two. Grave physical handicap which is so restricting that the individual cannot, even after due consideration and training, tolerate such a limited existence. This is fairly rare as a reason for suicide, despite the publicity surrounding [California cerebral palsy victim] Mrs. Elizabeth Bouvia's court cases.

What are the ethical parameters for autoeuthanasia?

A) *Being a mature adult.* That is essential. The exact age will depend on the individual.

B) *That it is clearly a considered decision.* You have to indicate this by such direct ways as belonging to a right to die society, signing a Living Will, signing a Durable Power of Attorney for Health Care. These documents do not give anybody freedom from criminality in assistance in suicide but they do indicate clearly, and in an authoritative way, what your intention was, and especially that this was not a hasty act.

C) *That the self-deliverance is not made at the first knowledge of the life-threatening illness and that reasonable medical help is sought.* We certainly do not believe in giving up the minute that you are informed that you are terminal, which is a common misconception of critics.

18

D) *That the treating physician has been informed and his response taken into account.* What his response will be depends on the circumstances of course, but we advise our members that as autoeuthanasia (or rational suicide) is not a crime there is nothing a doctor can do about it. But it is best to inform him and hear his response. You might well be mistaken—perhaps you misheard or misunderstood the diagnosis. Usually you will meet a discreet silence.

E) *Have made a will disposing of your worldly effects.* This shows evidence of a tidy mind and an orderly life; again, something which is paramount in rational suicide.

F) *Make plans to exit this life which do not involve others in criminal liability.* As I mentioned earlier, assistance in suicide is a crime, albeit a rarely punished crime, and certainly the most compassionate of all crimes. Very few cases ever come before the courts. . . .

G) *Leave a note saying exactly why you are self-destructing.* Also, as an act of politeness, if the act of self-destruction is done in a hotel, leave a note of apology to the staff for inconvenience and embarrassment caused. Some people, because of the criminality of assistance in suicide, don't want to put their loved ones through any risk, will leave home, go down the road, check into a hotel and take their life. . . .

Other Considerations

But, having considered the logic in favor of autoeuthanasia, the person should also address the countervailing arguments: . . .

[One] consideration is the question: does suffering ennoble? Is suffering a part of life and a preparation for death? Our response here is that if that is your firm belief then you are not a candidate for voluntary euthanasia. It is not an option ethically.

But we should remember that in America there are millions of agnostics and atheists and people of varying religions and denominations and they have rights too. We know that a good 50 percent of the Hemlock Society members are strong Christians and churchgoers, and that the God they worship is a God of love and understanding. As long as their autoeuthanasia was justifiable and met the conditions of not hurting other people then they feel that their God would accept them into heaven.

Another consideration is whether, by taking your life before the illness runs its full course, you are depriving yourself of a valuable period of good life, and also depriving your family and friends of your love and companionship. Here again, there is a great deal of misunderstanding about our point of view and what actually happens.

Practitioners of active voluntary euthanasia almost always wait to a late state in the dying process; some even wait too long and go into a coma and are frustrated in a self-deliverance. . . .

From my years in the Hemlock Society, hearing the feedback of hundreds, maybe thousands, of cases, I can assure you that most euthanasists do enjoy life, love living, and their feeling for the sanctity of life is as strong as anybody's. Yet they are willing to make a bargain if their dying is distressing to them to forego a few weeks of the end and leave under their own control.

The Comfort of Control

What is also not generally realized in the field of euthanasia is that, for many people, just knowing how to kill themselves is in itself of great comfort and often extends lives. Once a person knows how to make his/her exit and has the means, he/she will often renegotiate the conditions of dying.

An example was a Hemlock member in his nineties who called up and told me his health was so bad he was ready to terminate his life. He ordered and purchased the latest edition of *Let Me Die Before I Wake*, Hemlock's book on how to kill yourself, and called back a week or so later to say that he had got a friend in Europe to provide him with a lethal overdose. So everything was in position.

Euthanasia Will Be Legal

Thousands of dying patients in America would be comforted to know that, if and when their suffering becomes intolerable, a humane alternative is available to them. Many of us believe that it is inevitable that such an arrangement will come; there are simply too many patients who do not wish to languish in such hopeless situations and will take the measures to preclude such pointless suffering, not to mention the many physicians who believe that the current level of suffering is barbaric.

Ralph Mero in *Hemlock's Cup*, 1993.

"Where do you stand now?" I asked cautiously. "Oh, I'm not ready to go yet," he replied. Now that he had the means to make his exit, he was convinced that he could hold on longer. Thus, with the control and choice in his grasp, he had negotiated new terms concerning his fate.

Surely for those who want it this way this is commendable and is in fact an extension rather than a curtailment of life. . . .

Helping another to die in carefully considered circumstances is part of good medicine and also demonstrates a caring society that offers euthanasia to hopelessly sick persons as an act of love.

"Active euthanasia is never morally justified."

Euthanasia
Is Unethical

Ronald Otremba

Life is valuable, and to end it through euthanasia is unethical,
Ronald Otremba writes in the following viewpoint. While ill
people can ethically choose to refuse medical treatment,
Otremba believes they cannot ethically choose to take their own
lives. The author concludes that if the terminally ill were allowed to commit suicide, gradually society would allow others—
the handicapped, for example—to kill themselves. Otremba is
the director of Hospice HealthEast at St. Joseph's Hospital in St.
Paul, Minnesota.

As you read, consider the following questions:

1. On what principle does Otremba base his belief that all life is
   valuable?
2. How does the decision to end treatment differ from the
   decision to end one's life, in the author's view?
3. Why does Otremba believe that people should not be allowed
   to decide for themselves when life is no longer worth living?

Ronald Otremba, "Is Active Euthanasia Justifiable?" In *Active Euthanasia, Religion, and the
Public Debate*, 1991; a publication of the Park Ridge Center, Chicago, Illinois. Reprinted
with permission.

Is active euthanasia ever morally justified for patients who are terminally ill and who request either orally or through a written directive to have their lives ended? My answer to that question would have to be an unequivocal "no." Active euthanasia is never morally justified. On what basis do I make this decision? First, there is the principle that life itself is intrinsically valuable. This value is independent of one's physical or mental state of health. It is based on the principle that God is the sole creator of life and has sovereign authority over life and death. To some, this principle may seem cruel and unsympathetic, but it is, on the contrary, very respectful of the individual's needs and dignity. No matter what the condition of a person's life, there is still value in it. Value is not predicated on physical, emotional, economic, or social status but by the mere fact that one is human. This principle also gives us a reference for looking at two other principles related to the issue of active euthanasia—the principle of autonomy and the principle of burden/benefit.

The principle of autonomy states that the individual has a right to self-determination. This principle is not absolute but is subject to a higher authority or good. In application, the individual has the right to determine any treatment decision affecting his or her life. The individual patient has the right to request treatment, refuse treatment, or even terminate treatment once started.

Ending Treatment vs. Ending Life

Such autonomy is considered moral even if the decision means that one's life may be shortened by it. What is not moral is the decision to have one's life actively terminated. How does the decision to terminate treatment differ from the decision to end one's life when the outcomes are the same? In the first, death would most likely occur without treatment and possibly even in spite of treatment. It is possible to view the treatment as an intrusion or an undue burden in this case. In the second, the action itself can be viewed as a direct intrusion with the sole intent to end that person's life. There is a distinct difference between the two.

Just as autonomy has limits, so does burden/benefit. Treatment that would pose an undue burden on an individual does not have to be rendered. Treatment that has already been started can be stopped when it appears that the burden of the treatment outweighs the benefit that one hopes to achieve. It goes hand in hand with the individual's right to choose. The principle does not imply, however, that if life becomes burdensome, it can be terminated. Who determines when life becomes burdensome? The individual, the physician, society? What standards would be used if the individual were to choose? They would be totally subjective and relative to whatever circumstances the person found himself in. For one it might be a state of quadriplegia or the loss of a limb; for another it might be terminal illness, for another the loss of a loved one, and for still another, just the fear of being a burden. If active euthanasia were allowed on the basis of life's being unduly burdensome, each of the above circumstances could qualify; each could be considered so burdensome that death would seem a relief. Based on that reasoning, life would no longer have an intrinsic value but one subject to the changing tides of feelings and circumstances. If one were to have complete autonomy, one could choose to end one's life or to dictate that one's life be ended at any time and for whatever reason. Without limits, autonomy as well as burden/benefit would be subject to misuse and abuse in the form of relativism.

The Slippery Slope

In regard to selective euthanasia, we must be concerned with what the next step is likely to be. Societies always tend to expand the number of conditions and groups targeted for this "special treatment" or "final solution," and I agree with the concerns . . . about the impact of medically sanctioned suicide on the poor and handicapped.

C. Everett Koop, *Let's Talk*, 1992.

My obligation as a physician is, first and foremost, to practice within the guidelines of my faith and, second, to practice within the guidelines of my chosen profession. I am dedicated to the care of the total patient: to cure disease when possible, to alleviate pain and suffering as best I'm able, and to respect the dignity of the human person no matter how undignified his or her state of life may be.

Allowing active euthanasia, even though it be at the patient's request, would violate not only the principles of my faith but those of the practice of medicine as well.

"Whether it is in someone's best interests that his life end in one way rather than another depends on . . . his own sense of his integrity and critical interests."

Individuals Must Choose for Themselves Whether Euthanasia Is Ethical

Ronald Dworkin

People vary greatly in their views on what makes life meaningful, at what point life is no longer worth living, and how death should occur, Ronald Dworkin states in the following viewpoint. Consequently, while an athlete might find life as a quadriplegic worthless, an intellectual might find the same existence manageable and fulfilling. Similarly, some people view death as preferable to life in a vegetative state, while others believe that even permanently unconscious persons should be kept alive. Because of these differences, Dworkin believes that only individuals themselves can determine if and when euthanasia is ethical. Dworkin is a law professor at New York University and University Professor of Jurisprudence at Oxford University.

As you read, consider the following questions:

1. What role does timing play in a "good" death, according to Dworkin?
2. For what reasons does the author oppose laws addressing euthanasia?

Every day, rational people all over the world plead to be allowed to die. Sometimes they plead for others to kill them. Some of them are dying already, many in great pain, like Lillian Boyes, a seventy-year-old Englishwoman who was dying from a terrible form of rheumatoid arthritis so painful that even the most powerful painkillers left her in agony, screaming when her son touched her hand with his finger. Some of them want to die because they are unwilling to live in the only way left open to them, like Patricia Diane Trumbull, a forty-five-year-old New Yorker suffering from leukemia who refused chemotherapy and bone-marrow transplants, even though she was told the treatment would give her a one-in-four chance of surviving, because she knew the ravages of the treatment and did not think the odds good enough to endure it. Or Janet Adkins, a fifty-four-year-old Oregonian who knew she was in the early stages of Alzheimer's disease and wanted to die while she was still able to arrange it. Sometimes relatives plead for a family member to be allowed to die because the patient herself is in a permanent vegetative state, like Nancy Cruzan, whose cerebral cortex was destroyed by lack of oxygen after an accident, and whose life support was finally terminated in 1990, after she had lived for seven years as a vegetable, and after her parents had been to the Supreme Court and back. . . .

Death's Meaning

We cannot think about whether death is in someone's best interests unless we understand this dimension of the interests people have. It would be easy to decide whether it was in the best interests of Lillian Boyes or Nancy Cruzan or Janet Adkins to live or die if we had only their experiential interests [that is, what they could expect to experience in the future] in mind. Lillian Boyes had only pain to look forward to, and no pleasurable experiences that could possibly compensate for its experiential horror, so it was plainly in her interests, measured that way, to die as soon as possible. Nancy Cruzan would never have any experience, good or bad, again, so her experiential interests would not be affected by a decision either way. Janet Adkins probably had more to gain in pleasant experience by living on until a natural death—she would have remained capable of simple pleasures for several years, and many demented people do not suffer at all—so she was wrong to kill herself when she did if her experiential life was all that mattered. . . .

If we accept the view that only experiential interests count, we can make no sense of the widespread, near universal, view that decisions like those we have been reviewing are often personally problematic and racking. We agonize about these decisions, for ourselves when we are contemplating living wills, or for relatives and friends, only or mainly because we take our and their critical interests into account. We must therefore begin by asking: how does it matter to the critical success of our whole life how we die? We should distinguish between two different ways that it might matter: because death is the far boundary of life, and every part of our life, including the very last, is important; and because death is special, a peculiarly significant event in the narrative of our lives, like the final scene of a play, with everything about it intensified, under a special spotlight. In the first sense, when we die is important because of what will happen to us if we die later; in the second, how we die matters because it is how we *die*.

Let us begin with the first, less theatrical, of these ideas. Sometimes people want to live on, even though in pain or dreadfully crippled, in order to do something they believe important to have done. They want to finish a job, for example, or to learn something they have always wanted to know. Gareth Evans, a brilliant philosopher who died of cancer at the age of thirty-four, struggled to work on his unfinished manuscript as long as medicine could keep him in a condition in which he could work at all. Many people want to live on, as long as they can, for a more general reason: so long as they have any sense at all, they think, just being alive is *something*. Though Philip Roth had persuaded his eighty-six-year-old father to sign a living will, he hesitated when his father was dying and the doctors asked whether Roth wanted him put on a respirator. Roth thought, "How could I take it on myself to decide that my father should be finished with life, life which is ours to know just once?"

A Question of Dignity

On the other hand, people often think they have strong reasons of a comparable kind for *not* staying alive. The badness of the experiences that lie ahead is one: terrible pain or constant nausea or the horror of intubation or the confusions of sedation. When Roth thought about the misery to come, he whispered, "Dad, I'm going to have to let you go." But people's reasons for wanting to die include critical reasons as well; many people think it undignified or bad in some other way to live under certain conditions, however they might feel if they feel at all. Many people do not want to be remembered living in those circumstances; others think it degrading to be wholly dependent, or to be the object of continuing anguish. These feelings are often expressed as a distaste for causing trouble, pain, or expense to others, but the aversion is not fully captured in that other-regarding preference. It may be just as strong when the burden of physical care is imposed on professionals whose career is precisely in providing such care, and when the financial burden falls on a public eager to bear it. At least part of what people fear about dependence is its impact not on those responsible for their care, but on their own dignity.

I must emphasize that this is *not* a belief that every kind of dependent life under severe handicaps is not worth living. That belief is disproved not only by dramatic examples, like the brilliant life of Stephen Hawking, the almost wholly paralyzed cosmologist, but by the millions of ordinary people throughout the world who lead engaged, valuable lives in spite of appalling handicaps and dependencies. It is, however, plausible, and to many people compelling, that total dependence is in itself a very bad thing, quite apart from the pain or discomfort it often but not invariably entails. Total or near-total dependence with nothing positive to redeem it may seem not only to add nothing to the overall quality of a life but to take something important from it. That seems especially true when there is no possibility even of understanding that care has been given, or of being grateful for it. . . .

A Humane Choice

I would support active euthanasia and even some selected cases of physician-assisted suicides with the awareness and participation of the dying person and his or her family and closest friends. . . . Even if some choose to interpret the final act of dying to belong only to the divine giver of life, the human *has* control until it is wrested from him or her. The passion to control the destiny of others, even if morally justified and necessary, cannot be allowed to eclipse this foundational area of human dignity. . . . We must in my view be able humanely to support euthanasia requested by patients and surrogates.

Joseph Edelheit, *Active Euthanasia, Religion, and the Public Debate*, 1991.

When patients remain conscious, their sense of integrity and of the coherence of their lives crucially affects their judgment about whether it is in their best interests to continue to live. Athletes, or others whose physical activity was at the center of their self-conception, are more likely to find a paraplegic's life intolerable. . . . For such people, a life without the power of motion is unacceptable, not for reasons explicable in experiential terms, but because it is stunningly inadequate to the conception of self around which their own lives have so far been constructed. Adding decades of immobility to a life formerly organized around action will for them leave a narrative wreck, with no structure or sense, a life worse than one that ends when its activity ends.

Others will have radically different senses of self, of what has been critically important to their own lives. Many people, for example, would want to live on, almost no matter how horrible their circumstances, so long as they were able to read, or understand if read to them, the next day's newspaper. They would want to hear as many chapters as possible of the many thousands of stories about science and culture and politics and society that they had been following all their lives. People who embrace that newspaper test have assumed, and cannot easily disown, that part of the point of living is to know and care how things are turning out.

Death Must Reflect One's Life

So people's views about how to live color their convictions about when to die, and the impact is intensified when it engages the second way in which people think death is important. There is no doubt that most people treat the manner of their deaths as of special, symbolic importance: they want their deaths, if possible, to express and in that way vividly to confirm the values they believe most important to their lives. That ancient hope is a recurrent theme of Shakespearean drama. (Siward, for example, learning that Macbeth has killed Young Siward at Dunsinane in that poor boy's first battle, says: "Had I as many sons as I have hairs, I would not wish them to a fairer death.") When the great British political columnist Peter Jenkins realized on his deathbed that any conversation might be his last, he insisted on talking, though his nurses warned him not to, and on talking about political philosophy and the latest threats to free speech.

The idea of a good (or less bad) death is not exhausted by how one dies—whether in battle or in bed—but includes timing as well. It explains the premium people often put on living to "see" some particular event, after which the idea of their own death seems less tragic to them. A woman dying of cancer, whose life can be prolonged though only in great pain, might think she had good reason to live until the birth of an expected grandchild, or a long-awaited graduation, or some other family milestone. The aim of living not just until, but actually for, an event has very great expressive power. It confirms, in a fashion much exploited by novelists and dramatists, the critical importance of the values it identifies to the patient's sense of his own integrity, to the special character of his life. If his has been a life rooted in family, if he has counted, as among the high peaks of his life, family holidays and congresses and celebrations, then stretching his life to include one more such event does not merely add to a long list of occasions and successes. Treating the next one as salient for death confirms the importance of them all.

Many people have a parallel reason for wanting to die if an unconscious, vegetable life were all that remained. For some, this is an understandable worry about how they will be remembered. But for most, it is a more abstract and self-directed concern that their death, whatever else it is like, express their conviction that life has had value because of what life made it possible for them to do and feel. They are horrified that their death might express, instead, the opposite idea, which they detest as a perversion: that mere biological life—just hanging on—has independent value. Nietzsche said, "In a certain state it is indecent to live longer. To go on vegetating in cowardly dependence on physicians and machinations, after the meaning of life, the right to life, has been lost, that ought to prompt a profound contempt in society." He said he wanted "to die proudly when it is no longer possible to live proudly." That concern might make no sense for unconscious patients in a world where everyone treated the onset of permanent unconsciousness as itself the event of death, the final curtain after which nothing else is part of the story. But in such a world, no one would be kept alive in permanent unconsciousness anyway. No one would need worry, as many people in our world do, that others will feed or care for his vegetating body with what he believes the ultimate insult: the conviction that they do it for *him*.

The Most Important Choice

The awesome decision to live or die belongs not to the courts, to attorneys, to hospitals, to doctors, to nurses, or to any other group, but to the person whose life it is. The support of others is vital for an informed decision, so family, friends, and professionals can be of help, since they can help in the individual's free choice. And the most important choice one ever has is between life and death.

Arnold Beisser, *A Graceful Passage*, 1990.

The relatives who visit permanently unconscious patients regularly, and feel uncomfortable or anxious when they cannot, do not necessarily have that conviction. They come because they cannot bear not to see and touch someone they love so long as that is possible and not bad for him, and because they think that closing the final door before he is biologically dead and buried or cremated—before they can *mourn* him—would be a terrible betrayal, a declaration of indifference rather than the intense concern they still feel. There is no contradiction, but great force and sense, in the views of parents who fight, in court if

29

necessary, to have life support terminated but who will not leave their child's side until it is. But some people do believe that it *is* in a patient's best interests to be kept alive as long as possible, even in an unconscious state. For such people, contemplating themselves in that position, integrity delivers a very different command. The struggle to stay alive, no matter how hopeless or how thin the life, expresses a virtue central to *their* lives, the virtue of defiance in the face of inevitable death. It is not just a matter of taste on which people happen to divide, as they divide about surfing or soccer. None of us wants to end our lives out of character.

Now we can better answer the question of why people think what they do about death, and why they differ so dramatically. Whether it is in someone's best interests that his life end in one way rather than another depends on so much else that is special about him—about the shape and character of his life and his own sense of his integrity and critical interests—that no uniform collective decision can possibly hope to serve everyone even decently. So we have that reason of beneficence, as well as reasons of autonomy, why the state should not impose some uniform, general view by way of sovereign law but should encourage people to make provision for their future care themselves, as best they can, and why if they have made no provision the law should so far as possible leave decisions in the hands of their relatives or other people close to them whose sense of their best interests—shaped by intimate knowledge of everything that makes up where their best interests lie—is likely to be much sounder than some universal, theoretical, abstract judgment born in the stony halls where interest groups maneuver and political deals are done.

"No one's life is simply his or her own."

Euthanasia Cannot Be an Ethical Individual Choice

Gilbert Meilaender

In the following viewpoint, Gilbert Meilaender argues that both euthanasia and physician-assisted suicide are unethical because they involve "the choice of death." Moreover, he rejects the common argument that euthanasia is justified on the basis of personal autonomy—the idea that individuals have the right to make decisions concerning their own life and death. Meilaender cites various political theorists and religious traditions to support his assertion that people are not autonomous beings, but social creatures whose ethical responsibility toward society is violated by acts of self-destruction. Meilaender is a professor of religion at Oberlin College in Ohio.

As you read, consider the following questions:

1. Why are the two most commonly cited arguments for euthanasia unacceptable, according to Meilaender?
2. What does the author fear might happen if society accepts the belief that people have personal autonomy over their bodies?
3. Why is legalized euthanasia more dangerous in a secular society than in a religious one, in Meilaender's opinion?

Excerpted from Gilbert Meilaender, "Human Equality and Assistance in Suicide," *Second Opinion*, April 1994. Reprinted with permission.

In North American society of the late twentieth century, assisted suicide as a form of mercy killing is rapidly gaining social support. And although technical distinctions can be made between assisted suicide (helping someone take his or her own life) and euthanasia (directly taking the other person's life), it is clear that approval of the former would in fact be a step toward approval of the latter. Sue Rodriguez, a 42-year-old Canadian citizen suffering from Lou Gehrig's disease, recently petitioned the Supreme Court of Canada, asking that she be permitted the option of physician-assisted suicide at whatever point her condition becomes to her unbearable. Her request was only narrowly denied by a 5-4 vote of the court. In the state of Michigan Dr. Jack Kevorkian has made a practice of providing the gadgetry needed for people to take their lives—and has done so even in the face of a hastily passed law prohibiting assisted suicide in Michigan. Moreover, even though his procedures do not meet standards recommended by others who support assisted suicide and euthanasia, he has a reasonable amount of public sympathy and support.

Choosing Life, Choosing Death

This is, quite possibly, the next moral issue that will demand public attention, and in the United States it may even replace abortion as the most divisive of our "cultural" arguments. But it is not simply an argument about public policy; rather it involves and reveals our understanding of human nature. I focus here on assisted suicide, although the same issues are involved in the wider-ranging discussion of euthanasia. But we need to emphasize at the outset what is often not understood: We are not talking about decisions to withdraw treatments when those treatments are either useless or excessively burdensome. To oppose assisted suicide and euthanasia is not the same as claiming that one must always fight to the last operation or last treatment. When we withdraw treatment for good reason, we do not choose death. We choose life. From among the life choices still open to us we choose a life perhaps shorter than it would be with other alternatives but free of treatments that are now useless or burdensome. We do not turn against life but against certain treatments. Assisted suicide and euthanasia, today often blandly termed assistance in dying, are different matters, for they involve not just the desire to die but the choice of death. However difficult it may sometimes be to apply such conceptual distinctions, they are essential to moral reflection. They guide us, and they also challenge us to think more carefully about the difference between what we aim at and what we accomplish in our action.

Most arguments supporting assisted suicide rest on two appeals: (1) the importance of personal autonomy, including even a choice for death, and (2) the need to relieve suffering when we can. These two criteria, taken together, are thought both to authorize assisted suicide and, at the same time, to set limits to the practice. On the one hand, assisted suicide is authorized if a suffering person autonomously requests such help. On the other hand, such authorization is limited to circumstances in which the person is suffering greatly and is still capable of self-determination.

As Daniel Callahan has noted, however, this twofold appeal is inherently unstable. The limits will not stay in place for long if we press either side of the argument. Suppose we take relief of suffering seriously as authorization for assistance in dying. Then we may find it hard to retain autonomy as a necessary criterion. For if suffering is so significant, if suffering ought to be relieved even by assisted suicide, if that's the kind of claim suffering gives us on the actions of others, how can we possibly justify restricting such relief only to those who are able autonomously to request it? Are self-determining, autonomous people the only human beings who suffer greatly? Hardly. And so the pressure to expand the class of candidates for assistance in dying must be very powerful indeed. And the movement from assisted suicide to non-voluntary euthanasia is almost inevitable.

Voluntary, but Wrong

Our society, basing its view primarily on the fundamental values of Judaism and Christianity, has always forbidden the taking of innocent life and has considered that act one of the most serious, if not the most serious, breaches of morality possible. That one requests to be killed does not eliminate the very sound basis for the prohibition. . . . There are more ways to violate a person than by violating his or her will, and even actions voluntarily consented to can still be wrong.

Stephen Sapp, *Active Euthanasia, Religion, and the Public Debate*, 1991.

We might also press the other criterion, respect for autonomy. If we possess our life the way we possess other things, if we have a right to determine even when that life should end and a right to seek help in ending it, if human autonomy extends that far, why should the exercise of such a right be restricted to those who are suffering greatly? Might there not be other reasons why self-determining persons would wish to end their life and seek help in doing so? And once again, from this side of the argument, there must be powerful pressure to expand the class of candidates for assisted suicide and euthanasia. The combination of arguments—thought both to authorize and simultaneously to limit assistance in dying—is inherently unstable. It will not carry the day. Indeed, it is really only the opening round in the arguments—and is, in truth, the proverbial camel's nose under the tent.

Where that nose pokes its way, the body will soon follow. . . .

Individual Rights and Society

The fundamental issue here concerns the relation of individuals to their communities—whether and when private visions of the good may be constrained by the larger society. This question is the stock-in-trade of political theorists, and I turn to several of them for help in exploring the claim of autonomy. . . .

The appeal to self-determination is often made simply, straightforwardly, and, I think, powerfully. "It's my life, and I've been making decisions about it for as long as I can remember. Why shouldn't I be the one to set the terms on which I leave it? And, still more, who are you, or who is the larger community, to impose your will in these matters on mine—when it's my life?" This is an argument—or perhaps simply an attitude—that comes quite naturally to us, an attitude to which any of us may sometimes be inclined. Because it comes so naturally, it is all the more in need of examination. In a provocative essay titled "The Obligation to Live for the State," Michael Walzer uses Sir William Blackstone, Aristotle, and Fidel Castro to explore the appeal to autonomy.

Blackstone, in his *Commentaries on the Laws of England*, writes as follows of suicide: "The law of England wisely and religiously considers that no man hath a power to destroy life, but by a commission from God, the author of it; and, as the suicide is guilty of a double offense, one spiritual, in invading the prerogative of the Almighty, and rushing into his immediate presence uncalled for; the other temporal, against the king, who hath an interest in the preservation of all his subjects; the law has therefore ranked this among the highest crimes." Clearly, Blackstone did not place self-determination first in the scale of moral values. He did not think of human beings as autonomous—for two reasons. Their lives belonged to God and to the earthly representative of God, the king. It may seem that neither reason has much standing in public discussion today. Belief in God has been, as we say, "privatized"—all right if that's how one feels about things, but removed from our common life. And the king has been democratized into a body of equals, each thought to be an autonomous, self-determining being.

The puzzle in all this, however, is that the view that my life is my own to do with as I please is held not only or chiefly by hard-core political libertarians; it is held also by those who on other occasions, when dealing with other issues, will condemn the "excessive individualism" of our society. And surely we need to remind ourselves that there are other ways to think about the constitution of the self. Individuals are not necessarily autonomous monads, at least not if the language of human solidarity is to carry any weight. Walzer cites a statement issued by Fidel Castro in 1964 after Augusto Martinez Sanchez, an official of the Cuban revolutionary government, had committed suicide: "We are deeply sorry for this event, although in accordance with elemental revolutionary principles, we believe this conduct by a revolutionary is unjustifiable and improper. . . . We believe that Comrade Martinez could not consciously have committed this act, since every revolutionary knows that he does not have the right to deprive his cause of a life that does not belong to him, and that he can only sacrifice against an enemy."

Blackstone would have understood. So would Aristotle, who writes in the *Nicomachean Ethics*:

> He who through anger voluntarily stabs himself does this contrary to the right rule of life, and this the law does not allow; therefore he is acting unjustly. But towards whom? Surely towards the state, not towards himself. For he suffers voluntarily, but no one is voluntarily treated unjustly. This is also the reason that the state punishes; a certain loss of civil rights attaches to the man who destroys himself, on the ground that he is treating the state unjustly.

Such a view would not, of course, entirely prohibit assisted suicide; instead, it would require public permission before one proceeded to the act. Thus, Emile Durkheim says, in Athens a citizen had to ask permission of the Senate before killing himself. If the request was granted, the suicide would be considered legitimate. That is, however, a far cry from our notion that these are essentially private decisions for which we are accountable to no one else.

To reflect upon the views of men as different as Blackstone, Castro, and Aristotle is to realize that the attitude I instinctively adopt about "my life" is not as obviously valid as it may seem. As a student of mine once put it in discussion, referring to an 18-year-old cousin of hers who had committed suicide and whose family had never been the same afterward: "He didn't just take his own life. He took part of theirs too."

The Social Self

The Western religious tradition has also presupposed a different vision of the self—as necessarily social and not ultimately autonomous. It has taught that no one's life is simply his or her own. For Jews and Christians, it is the Author of our being who has ultimate authority over it. To be sure, we are granted genuine freedom to make decisions that shape our life, a freedom sometimes so creative that it must be understood as a kind of participation in God's own creative power, but ours is always the freedom of a creature—and is, therefore, exercised up against the limit that is God. Without that limit it becomes simply a sea of infinite possibility, and we may be hard-pressed finally to find any reason for choosing one destination for our voyage rather than another—hard-pressed even to find any reason for trying to stay afloat. Such reasons require a background of intelligibility that is available only if our freedom has a ground and a limit. What might look like an even fuller freedom, grounded simply in itself, is more godlike than we can manage. Its ground will prove ultimately to be the void, and it will—as we are beginning to see—be destructive of human life, not creative of new possibilities. That is the price we will pay if we take the politically useful fiction of the autonomous individual and transform it into the moral basis of our entire life. Good politics and good ethics are not always the same. . . .

Equality and Freedom

In the movement toward assisted suicide, we are in danger of losing a central moral insight—namely, our fundamental equality as human beings. We can reflect upon the roots of that belief by considering its appearance in the thought of John Locke, one of the founders of our own tradition of political discourse.

In his *Second Treatise of Government* Locke contemplated the condition of human beings in a state of nature, free of any common power or authority, and he concluded that all would be morally equal. In such a state, wrote Locke,

> all the Power and Jurisdiction is reciprocal, no one having more than another: there being nothing more evident than that Creatures of the same species and rank . . . should also be equal one amongst another without Subordination or Subjection, unless the Lord and Master of them all, should by any manifest Declaration of his Will set one above another, and confer on him by an evident and clear appointment an undoubted Right to Dominion and Sovereignty.

In such a condition human beings were free, but they were also equal. And in Locke's understanding the equality set limits upon the freedom. The natural state of liberty is not, Locke says, a state of license. And in particular, no person, free and autonomous though he may be, has a moral right to take the life of another "unless it be to do Justice to an Offender." Precisely because all human beings are equal and independent, no one can be given or can exercise rightful dominion over the life of another; no person can properly possess the personhood of another.

Of course Locke knew that human beings do not necessarily seem equal when we consider their abilities and powers. And his assertion of human equality in the *Second Treatise* does not in fact rest upon such comparison of relative capacities. It is grounded instead in a picture of all human beings as equidistant from their Creator. Scholars may differ about how seriously Locke took such religious underpinnings, but his language is clear:

> For Men being all the Workmanship of one Omnipotent, and infinitely wise Maker; All the Servants of one Sovereign Master, sent into the World by his order and about his business, they are his Property, whose Workmanship they are, made to last during his, not one another's Pleasure. And being furnished with like Faculties, sharing all in one Community of Nature, there cannot be supposed any such Subordination among us, that may Authorize us to destroy one another, as if we were made for one another's uses, as the inferior ranks of Creatures are for ours.

Locke here raises for us an important question. Does the growing movement in support of physician-assisted suicide (and euthanasia) indicate that, having dispensed with God in our common life, we may also lose our commitment to human equality?

Responsibility to the State

The state considers life sacred; therefore, it has a compelling interest in preserving life. That position is based on an abstract concern that we should respect the sanctity of life. There is also an assumption that you as an individual have some contribution to make to society.

George M. Burnell, *Final Choices*, 1993.

The question arises from two angles—that of the person who seeks assistance in suicide and that of the person who offers it. Although I may sometimes rightly give my life for another, if I seek to give ultimate authority over my life to another I become less than human. For then I join Locke's "inferior ranks of Creatures," and I make my person an object to be possessed and controlled by another, and it is difficult to think of that other person as merely my equal. Likewise, the person who offers assistance in suicide "pulls rank" and, in effect, exercises a more-than-human authority. If I try to give into the hands of a fellow human being authority to take my life, I make of that person more than he is in truth—more than my equal.

A Godlike Act

Paradoxical as it may seem, physician-assisted suicide and euthanasia are more dangerous in a society that considers itself secular—a society like ours—than they would be in a society grounded in explicitly shared religious beliefs. We can see why if we consider an analogous argument made by Albert Camus about capital punishment. He suggested that the justice or injustice of the death penalty depended on the ultimate frame of reference within which it was used and understood. And he argued that capital punishment could be justified only where there was a socially shared belief that the final verdict on any person's life was not given in this world. Although his claim is likely to take us by surprise at first, it bears the mark of deep insight into the difference that belief in God makes within a culture. In a society where belief in God is widespread, to condemn a fellow human being to death need not involve divine pretension. Those who execute the verdict must know that, however necessary it seems to be, it does not constitute an ultimate judgment on the life of one who is their equal—a fellow human being. But what of a society that lacks such publicly acknowledged religious beliefs? In it, Camus thought, execution must mean elimination from the only human community whose existence all people grant. Hence, it would be a godlike act and could not express an understanding of human equality between executor and executed.

Camus does not, of course, intend to argue in defense of capital punishment. Rather, he opposes it precisely because, without belief in God, it must undercut our commitment to human equality; it cannot express a true humanism. And we, contemplating the different problem of assisted suicide, may wonder whether a true humanism can survive without the background beliefs that underlay Locke's argument.

We assume that it must be harder to make an argument against assisted suicide in a secular society—and in a sense, of course, it is, since there is less to limit our claims to autonomy. But I am suggesting that physician-assisted suicide may be an especially dangerous social practice in a society like ours. Such a practice undercuts the basis for true human equality by substituting for Locke's Creator some of our fellow human beings—those, presumably, with certain capacities still intact. And we pull rank by eliminating one of our equals from the only life that we all, by common acknowledgment, share. Autonomy, without the limit of equality, proves to be very lonely indeed. Some of us become gods; others join "the inferior ranks of Creatures." What we are not is equals who have a common life and support each other in the effort to live out our personal histories. If we do not think this a dangerously slippery slope, it may be only because we are already sliding too fast to think clearly.

> *"Mercy killing is proscribed as an unwarranted intervention in an area that must be governed only by God himself."*

Assisted Suicide Is Contrary to Judeo-Christian Beliefs

J. David Bleich

J. David Bleich is a professor of Talmud and director of the Postgraduate Institute for Jurisprudence and Family Law at the Rabbi Isaac Elchanan Theological Seminary in New York City. In the following viewpoint, Bleich argues that according to Judeo-Christian tradition, God is the creator of life, and only God can determine when life should end. Consequently, euthanasia—which is humankind's way of hastening death before God's time—is immoral. Bleich also maintains that every life contributes to the grandeur of God, and that the loss of one person—even a comatose person—lessens God's magnificence.

As you read, consider the following questions:

1. According to the Talmud, as quoted by Bleich, why was only a single human being created in the world?
2. Why is it wrong for people to make decisions concerning life and death based upon their own intellectual understanding, in the author's opinion?
3. How do people serve God, in Bleich's opinion?

Excerpted from J. David Bleich, "Life as an Intrinsic Rather Than Instrumental Good: The 'Spiritual' Case Against Euthanasia." Reprinted by permission of the publisher, from *Issues in Law & Medicine*, vol. 9, no. 2, Fall 1993. Copyright ©1993 by the National Legal Center for the Medically Dependent & Disabled, Inc.

"But your blood of your lives will I require; from the hand of every beast will I require it, and from the hand of man, from the hand of a person's brother, will I require the life of man." This earliest and most detailed biblical prohibition against homicide contains one phrase that is an apparent redundancy. Since the phrase "from the hand of man" pronounces man culpable for the murder of his fellow man, to what point is it necessary for Scripture to reiterate "from the hand of a person's brother will I require the life of man"? Fratricide is certainly no less heinous a crime than ordinary homicide. A nineteenth century biblical scholar, Rabbi Jacob Zevi Mecklenburg, in his commentary on the Pentateuch, *Ha-Ketav ve-ha-Kabbalah*, astutely comments that, while murder is the antithesis of brotherly love, in some circumstances the taking of the life of one's fellow man may be perceived as indeed being an act of love par excellence. Euthanasia, designed to put an end to unbearable suffering, is born not of hatred or anger but of concern and compassion. It is precisely the taking of life even under circumstances in which it is manifestly obvious that the perpetrator is motivated by feelings of love and brotherly compassion that the Bible finds necessary to brand as murder, pure and simple. Despite the noble intent that prompts such an action, mercy killing is proscribed as an unwarranted intervention in an area that must be governed only by God himself. The life of man may be reclaimed only by the Author of life. As long as man is yet endowed with a spark of life—as defined by God's eternal law—man dare not presume to hasten death, no matter how hopeless or meaningless continued existence may appear to be in the eyes of a mortal perceiver. . . .

The Value of One Life

The value of human life is supreme and takes precedence over virtually all other considerations. This attitude is most eloquently summed up in a Talmudic passage regarding the creation of Adam: "Therefore only a single human being was created in the world, to teach that if any person has caused a single soul to perish, Scripture regards him as if he had caused an entire world to perish; and if any human being saves a single soul, Scripture regards him as if he had saved an entire world." Human life is not a good to be preserved as a condition of other values but as an absolute, basic, and precious good in its own stead. The obligation to preserve life is commensurately all-encompassing.

Accordingly, life with suffering is regarded as being, in many cases, preferable to termination of life and with it elimination of suffering. . . .

The meaning and value of human life is a divine mystery. Man is commanded to procreate, to nurture and sustain life, and to preserve the life that has been entrusted to him until it is reclaimed by the Creator of all life. Whether or not man finds value in the life he is commanded to preserve is, in this fundamental sense, irrelevant; man's obligations vis-à-vis sustaining life are not predicated upon his aptitude for fathoming divine secrets.

Man must hearken to the divine command regardless of whether he understands its purpose or fails to do so, and, assuredly, he may not seek to rescind or modify the divine imperative on the plea that he does fathom the divine intent and is capable of independent decisionmaking in effecting its realization. Nevertheless, man is not constrained from endeavoring to ascertain purposes or values reflected in the divine command provided that he does not become guilty of hubris in allowing his intellect to substitute human norms for the divine imperative. . . .

Human Life and Divine Grandeur

In *Hales v. Petit*, a classic sixteenth century case in which the interest of the state in prevention of suicide was first articulated, Justice Dyer wrote that suicide is an offense "against the king in that hereby he has lost a subject, and . . . he being the head has lost one of his mystical members." Suicide may be prevented—and punished—by the king because it constitutes interference with his rights as monarch. . . . Royal majesty is perceived as a correlate of the number of subjects over whom the monarch reigns. The more citizens in his domain, the greater the king. Thus, to deprive the king of a subject is to diminish his grandeur; to willfully cause the death of a subject of the king is to be guilty of *lèse majesté*.

A Breach of Morality

Our society, basing its view primarily on the fundamental values of Judaism and Christianity, has always forbidden the taking of innocent life and has considered that act one of the most serious, if not the most serious, breaches of morality possible.

Stephen Sapp in *Active Euthanasia, Religion, and the Public Debate*, 1991.

Although this, too, is a mystery beyond our ken, God is the supreme King, whose dominion extends over all of mankind. The more numerous the populace, the greater is his grandeur. The loss of even a single life represents a diminution of his kingship. One of the most solemn prayers in the Jewish liturgy is the *Kaddish*, the mourner's prayer. Although recited as memorialization of a loved one, the *Kaddish* contains no reference to the deceased, no hint of reward or punishment, no mention of everlasting life, and no prayer for the repose of the soul of the departed. Its opening phrase, "May His great Name be magnified and sanctified," sets the tenor of the entire prayer as a paean celebrating ultimate universal acceptance of divine sovereignty. Rabbi Meir Shapiro of Lublin explained that the loss of even a single human life represents a diminution of divine sovereignty and hence evokes a prayer expressing the supplicant's yearning for the restoration and enhancement of God's glory.

It is difficult enough for us to comprehend any sense in which mere human existence serves to enhance the glory of the Deity. In anthropomorphic terms, we can readily understand that a monarch's power and glory, both real and perceived, are directly commensurate with the number of able-bodied, healthy, productive subjects over whom he rules. But incremental numbers of aged, nonproductive, ailing subjects hardly enhance royal power or grandeur. Nevertheless, to the extent that the mind can fathom the mystery of human existence, mankind must be perceived as constituting a vast orchestra engaged in a continuous performance in praise of the Creator. In an orchestra, each musician has an assigned role, and those assigned identical or similar roles are arranged in groups. There are separate sections for musicians playing wind, string, and percussion instruments. Not all the musicians and not all sections play at once. Effective rendition of the musical arrangement requires that, at times, some of the musicians remain silent. Yet even when not actually engaged in playing his instrument, every member remains seated with the orchestra and contributes to the visual magnificence of the performance. Similarly, each and every individual has an assigned role in the divine orchestration of mankind. Not every member is called upon to extol the Deity by fulfilling his assigned role continuously. Some, by virtue of their physical condition, may be quiescent; they are silent members of an orchestra that is nevertheless more majestic by virtue of their presence. Even though an individual in a precarious physical condition may not have the capacity to serve God in an active sense, nevertheless, his very existence constitutes an act of divine service.

Man as the Chattel of God

Preservation and prolongation of the life of a comatose patient also serve to impress a significant moral lesson upon the human conscience. Much is said in our day regarding patient autonomy and the right of every individual to be master of his or her own destiny. To be sure, no person enjoys rights over the life of another. Nevertheless, the concept of personal autonomy is flawed if it is understood as embodying the notion that man enjoys a proprietary interest in his own life. Our religious heritage teaches us that God is the Creator of man and that he is the Author of both life and death. Thus, even Plato spoke of man as the "chattel of the gods" in denying man's right to foreshorten his own life. Man's interest in his life and in his body are subservient to those of the Creator. It is extremely easy to lose sight of that verity, since, in the ordinary course of events, a person's natural desires, self-interest, and preservation instinct serve to assure that his natural inclinations coincide with his moral obligation. That is frequently not the case when a person is pain-ridden, debilitated, and terminally ill or involved in decisionmaking on behalf of a comatose or nonsentient patient. In such cases, preservation of life does not appear to be at all desirable from a human perspective. But precisely because there is no longer a human will to live does man become cognizant of the fact that he may not make a decision to terminate life because his autonomy is not untrammeled. He is forcibly reminded of the fact that it is the Creator who is the ultimate proprietor of human life—a lesson that man might otherwise be prone to forget.

6

"I would support active euthanasia. . . . I make this statement fully aware that life is a unique divine gift."

Assisted Suicide Is Not Contrary to Judeo-Christian Beliefs

Joseph Edelheit

Many of those who oppose euthanasia base their opposition on religious grounds. In the following viewpoint, Joseph Edelheit argues that although Jewish tradition demands that individuals choose life, medical advances and the AIDS pandemic require a reevaluation of the meaning of life and death. Edelheit concludes that euthanasia, in the context of modern society, is a humane option that is not contrary to Judeo-Christian beliefs. Edelheit is a congregational reform rabbi at Temple Emmanuel in Chicago.

As you read, consider the following questions:

1. What does Jewish tradition teach about life and death, according to the author?
2. Who should have control of euthanasia decisions, according to Edelheit?
3. What has the pandemic of AIDS forced society to recognize, according to the author?

Joseph Edelheit, "Is Active Euthanasia Justifiable?" In *Active Euthanasia, Religion, and the Public Debate*, 1991; a publication of the Park Ridge Center, Chicago, Illinois. Reprinted with permission.

The 1990s will demand of us a critical and often painful reflection on what we mean by life and death. We have spent nearly a century caught between the paradoxical poles of unthinkable acts of genocide and uncontrollable population growth. We have participated culturally in acts of violence which make death a senseless void, and we have engaged in scientific discoveries and medical technologies that have added measurably to both the quality and quantity of life. Given those highly charged paradoxical polarities, it is not coincidental that during the final decade of this century, we need to ask, What do we mean by life and death? The specific question of whether active euthanasia can be morally justified goes to the very core of how we will eventually understand what we mean by life and death.

Answering this question *today* presupposes our willingness to answer it *differently* as our understanding changes. The many variables in this area will determine the still emerging parameters of our answer. As a congregational Reform rabbi, I am acutely aware that my interpretation of Jewish tradition does not represent a "universal" Jewish answer, and my involvement as an AIDS activist has also given me a distinct bias. With these caveats in mind, I would support active euthanasia and even some selected cases of physician-assisted suicides with the awareness and participation of the dying person and his or her family and closest friends. I make this statement fully aware that life is a unique divine gift.

Choose Life . . . Unless

Jewish tradition teaches us that life and death are not passive, but active categories. One of the most quoted passages from Hebrew Scriptures is Deuteronomy 30:19, "I have set before you life and death, the blessing and the curse, therefore choose life that you may live—you and your seed." Lost in the translation from the Hebrew is the grammatical nuance, second person singular, for the imperative: choose life! *You*—as an individual—are required to choose life. Would Moses have used this dramatic peroration if there had been any indication that doctors, nurses, hospital administrators, nursing and convalescent home staffs, judges and lawyers could all choose for you? Within the biblical setting the definition of life was simple—breathing. We have long since passed that watershed of medical innocence. Were Moses speaking today, I pray he would charge us with a more relevant admonition—"Choose life . . . unless it is a machine!"

The key element of the question before us pertains to the assertive participation of the patients "who request to have their lives ended." Not only is there a public consensus—there is a strong indication that scripture allows us this final act of free will. Even if some choose to interpret the final act of dying to belong only to the divine giver of life, the human *has* control until it is wrested from him or her. The passion to control the destiny of others, even if morally justified and necessary, cannot be allowed to eclipse this foundational area of human dignity. To this end, we must continue to ask each other—what do we mean by life and death?

Hundreds of thousands are sick and dying, and millions will eventually die, from the pandemic of HIV/AIDS. This disease has forced us only now to begin to reckon with the profound link between sexuality and death. We have spent nearly 20 years in a national debate about abortion and choice—defending the rights of an unborn fetus and attempting to define when life begins. How curious that the lines separating "prochoice" and "prolife" cross and recross as the rhetoric becomes more sophisticated. The debates over abortion and euthanasia are already overlapping. How many people understand the words *prochoice*

and *prolife* and what they really mean? As a society, we are morally derelict if we do not answer the question regarding active euthanasia, but can we answer it without knowing and understanding what we mean by life and death?

The Living and the Dying

We must in my view be able humanely to support euthanasia requested by patients and surrogates, a goal that can be reached only by the difficult process of public conversation. Allow me to close with one final provocative question, intended to communicate the urgency of our conversation. An estimated 10,000 persons in America remain in persistent vegetative states and cannot die for various legal reasons. How can we justify this indignity to them and their families when we accept as nearly axiomatic the deaths of more than 20,000 persons—double the number of those in PVS—in wanton acts of urban violence with handguns? We can't seem to legislate a means to allow those who have no life to die, nor can we legislate a means to allow those who have life to live.

"Euthanasia for conscious, mentally competent patients—in a word, medicide—has now been eliminated as an ethical problem for the medical profession."

Physician-Assisted Suicide Is Ethical

Jack Kevorkian

Jack Kevorkian is well known for his mission to promote physician-assisted suicide and for his participation in more than twenty such suicides. Kevorkian is a retired Michigan pathologist. In the following viewpoint, excerpted from his book *Prescription: Medicide, the Goodness of Planned Death*, Kevorkian explains his belief that it is ethical for physicians to help patients commit suicide because death is caused not by the physician but by the individual patient, who alone is responsible for the morality of the act.

As you read, consider the following questions:

1. What is the difference between rule ethics and situation ethics, according to Kevorkian?
2. How does the author refute the slippery slope argument made by opponents of euthanasia?
3. How has medical progress brought changes in medical ethics, according to Kevorkian?

Reprinted from Jack Kevorkian's *Prescription: Medicide* with permission from Prometheus Books, Buffalo, New York.

A legitimate, comprehensive, and universally valid code of medical ethics no longer exists. In fact, it never did.

What has traditionally passed for "ethics" among doctors is a vague body of unwritten rules of obscure origin that loosely prescribes professional etiquette among themselves and for their relationship with patients. This seemed to be enough in the days of rudimentary medicine, when the doctors' carefully nurtured aura of godliness reinforced the psychological impact of their herbal concoctions for superstitious patients.

New Rules Are Needed

But today's modern patients expect much more. Now stripped of self-assumed sanctimony, many doctors are almost panicking because the old rules don't work any more. The once haughty healers now look to the law, to clerics, to a growing army of latter-day ethicists, to hastily contrived ethics committees, and even to the public for guidance on when, how, and why to use the awesome power modern science and technology have placed at their disposal.

Ask any doctor why he or she does or does not do certain things in certain ways and chances are you'll hear the words "Hippocratic Oath." Then ask what that oath is, and be prepared for a few confident replies amid a welter of stammering and poorly disguised guessing. Next, ask the confident ones where the oath came from, and observe how, with diminishing confidence, they will tell you that it was formulated by Hippocrates in ancient Greece; fewer still may add that he lived in Cos in the fifth century B.C.

For the majority of doctors, especially those over the age of fifty, and for me until very recently, the oath was something occasionally mentioned in medical school but rarely studied in detail. Even casual comments about it never seemed to go beyond a few selective clichés. I never took the oath, and as far as I know it was never officially administered to my graduating class in 1952 at the University of Michigan. Indeed, it is now uncommon for any American medical faculty to insist that the oath be taken by graduating doctors. That alone renders suspect the hallowed oath's importance or relevance to modern medical practice. . . .

A New Approach to Ethics

Ethical vacuum—that's the root of the problem. Doctors have got to come to grips with the realities of the times and fill that vacuum with a code of conduct tailored to meet the contemporary demands. And that calls for wrenching the profession entirely free of so-called *rule ethics*. According to philosopher-theologian Joseph Fletcher, rule ethics mandates *a priori* what one must do "according to some predetermined precept or categorical imperative." It is a coercive, nondiscriminatory, "doctrinaire or ideological method of deciding what is right." On the other hand, *situation ethics* is *a posteriori*, "relative, flexible, and changeable according to variables (from which) the moral agent, the decision maker, judges what is best in the circumstances and in the view of foreseeable consequences."

Judge Amnon Carmi of the Society for Medicine and Law in Haifa, Israel, shares this ethical stance, which ennobles human dignity by giving free reign to "the ability of man to think things over, to decide, and to apply self-control, to become his own master. . . . It is the sense of worth that comes with having the freedom and responsibility to make judgments about what is proper and improper."

Fletcher anticipated the medical relevance of the situational approach, which to some physicians is simply "clinical" ethics independent of strictly moral rules. If the medical profession has any residual sense of worth, it should enthusiastically and unconditionally embrace this only workable guide to the use of reason and common sense in searching for solutions to modern ethical questions.

Those now in control of society's destiny are against my proposals simply because they cannot escape some "eternal truths" of religion or of their own rigid and unreflective opinions. They cannot distinguish rule ethics from situation (or casuistic) ethics.

The Weakness of the Slippery Slope Argument

One of the most powerful forces energizing the rule approach is fear of the so-called wedge or slippery slope (also known as the camel's nose under the tent, a foot in the door, and give an inch . . .) argument. All of these catchwords imply eventual moral disaster through supposedly inevitable abuse of any "radical" innovation, no matter how small or innocuous its beginning. This dread of gray zones and of imaginative novelty ultimately rests on a lack of confidence in one's ability to control—and is, in effect, an admission of character weakness.

It is absurd and degrading to offer this fear as though it were a rationally persuasive argument. That point was made by the President's Commission for the Study of Ethical Problems in Medicine, which concluded that "much more is needed than merely pointing out that allowing one kind of action (itself justified) could conceivably increase the tendency to allow another action (unjustified). Rather, it must be shown that pressures to allow the unjustified action will become so strong once the initial step is taken that the further steps are likely to occur . . . (and) such evidence is commonly quite limited." Even the fear of abuse can be (and often is) abused. In its 1983 report the President's Commission warned that "slippery slope arguments are themselves subject to abuse in social and legal policy debate." If successfully foisted on society, extreme degrees of neophobia could result only in complete stagnation and ineluctable backsliding. . . .

Physicians Can Now Be Protected

No longer is there a need—or even an excuse—for anyone to be the direct mediator of the death of another who is alert, rational, and who for some compelling reason chooses to, or must, die. Performance of that repulsive task should now be relegated exclusively to a device like the Mercitron, which the doomed subject must activate. [Ed. note: The Mercitron is a device invented by Kevorkian that provides a lethal intravenous solution to assist people in suicide.] What is most important is that the participation of doctors or other health professionals now becomes strictly optional, either to insert a needle into the subject's vein to start the harmless saline infusion, or to monitor an ECG tracing to verify and document the occurrence of death. A doctor no longer need perform the injection.

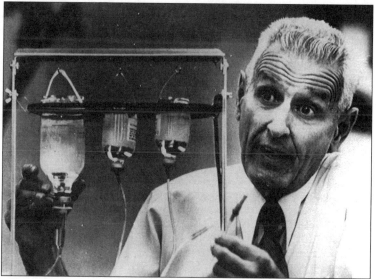

AP/ Wide World.

Such indirect and innocuous (and to some extent even beneficial) medical conduct concentrates any question of morality only, and squarely, on the patient. Morality thus so absolutely

51

subjectivized is hopelessly immune to justifiable extraneous (or objective) assessment. In other words, it is wrong for any and all members of society to even try to judge the morality of an individual's action, deemed by that society to be immoral, when the individual concerned disagrees and performs the action in such a manner as not to infringe the autonomy of others or society's official rules of culpability.

Euthanasia for conscious, mentally competent patients—in a word, medicide—has now been eliminated as an ethical problem for the medical profession. . . .

Progress Yields Changes in Ethics

Traditionally the mission of a healer has been to ease pain and suffering as well as to preserve and restore health and, as corollaries, to facilitate birth and to postpone death. The latter two cardinal events mark off what I call the "visible spectrum" of medicine, the components of which fluctuated very little if at all from antiquity to the recent past.

In view of the early rudimentary knowledge of human biology with its plethora of herbs and drugs having little or no efficacy, of fanciful dietary regimens, of a few crude surgical procedures, and the psychological impact of doctors' priestly aura, it is understandable why the amplitude and intensity of that "visible spectrum" remained relatively invariable and small for many centuries. Throughout the world, human beings of all ages were constantly at the mercy of crippling and lethal diseases occurring sporadically or as devastating plagues, and against which a weak medical arsenal had very little to offer. In such bleak circumstances it is no small wonder that a desperate humanity would rank the maintenance and prolongation of life to be medicine's primary mission.

Other less mundane but equally important factors were involved in the establishment of that priority in the Western world. Perhaps the most powerful was the inflexible and harshly punitive Judeo-Christian dogma that espoused the absolute and inviolable "sanctity" of human life. Reinforcing that was the medieval necessity for powerful emperors and feudal lords to keep their personal combat forces adequately manned. Among the inevitable consequences of all this were the taboos against abortion, suicide, and euthanasia. Vestiges of those taboos have endured to our "enlightened" time.

The ironclad morality of such arbitrary rule ethics began to crack under the pressure of scientific, demographic, economic, and social changes. The rate of increase of population and of living standards became geometric as a result of advances in medical capabilities, in public health, and in the industrial transformation of agrarian cultures. These in turn secularized society and vitiated theistic absolutism. The ensuing pressures led to official breach of two of the taboos mentioned above. Within the last century the common law crime of suicide has been annulled; the act is no longer illegal. Abortion and birth control, too, have been legitimized, albeit intermittently and with limitations. No matter what legal or religious injunctions are imposed in the foreseeable future, these two taboos will never again withstand the evolving pressures of contrary demand. (The Prohibition fiasco should be lesson enough.)

Kevorkian as Rescuer

It's not easy to die, even if you want to and even if you're terminally ill. A huge number of the right kind of pills will work, but not everyone that sick can swallow, or even move. Such people who want to die need help. (And, just as important, people who fear the torture disease can bring need just to know such help would be there.)

Dr. Kevorkian—first with his "suicide machine" and later, when the courts took that away from him, with a tankful of carbon monoxide—has rescued such people. I say "rescued" because I know from experience how someone feels who wants to die and can't—like an animal in a trap. My mother used that word—a horrible word, not only because of the pain it implies but because of the terror of being helpless in the face of torture.

Betty Rollin, *Family Circle*, April 26, 1994.

The breaking of the stranglehold on practices of abortion and birth control not only enhanced one extreme of medicine's "visible spectrum" but also helped expand it into the previously unimagined and even unthinkable "ultrabirth" realm. An overdue lenity paved the way for the application of increasingly sophisticated techniques of modern science and technology in the evolution of a new specialty called fetology, and in expanding the frontiers of embryology. It is in this currently "invisible ultrabirth" part of the biological spectrum (analogous to the invisible ultraviolet component of the physical electromagnetic spectrum) that the promise of so-called genetic engineering will be realized. From the ashes of a shattered taboo will have arisen the best possible means to search for the cure or prevention of countless genetic and hereditary diseases—and even perhaps to preprogram every human conceptus for a long life of guaranteed biological integrity.

The time has come to smash the last irrational and most fearsome taboo of planned death and thereby to open the floodgates of equally momentous benefit for humankind. In the first place, the positive euthanasia of obitiatry [Kevorkian's term for the medical speciality concerned with "the treatment or doctoring of death"] would expand enormously the amplitude and intensity of the ordinary "visible spectrum." It would do this by allowing doctors for the first time to carry out on living human beings otherwise impossible trials of new and untested drugs, devices, or operations. That would accelerate medical progress by eliminating the need for experiments on animals or on ill patients who volunteer to be test subjects. But the biggest impact of obitiatry will probably be its extension of the abstract spectrum of medicine into the opposite "invisible infradeath" realm, where the real potential for serious investigation of the phenomenon of death is to be found. . . .

Obitiatry . . . should be legitimized and implemented as soon as possible; but that calls for the strident advocacy of influential personalities who, unfortunately, choose to remain silent or disinterested—or simply antithetical.

My lone voice cannot accomplish much. But in having taken action through the practice of medicide as the first step in the right direction, I have done all that I can possibly do on behalf of a just cause for our species. I have no delusions about the end result of it all. If the lessons of history are still valid, then my evanescent proposal will quickly disappear in the infinity of time, only to be revived every millennium or two by some naive individual whose delight in having such a beneficial "original" idea inevitably will give way to the despair of futility in trying to promulgate it. By comparison, my despair will have been mild and short-lived.

But who knows—there's always the chance that some unexpected quirk of human nature will compel a generally misguided society to add a new twist to the lessons of history by doing the right thing (for a change) at the right time and instituting obitiatry without qualms and without delay.

Who knows?

> *"Life is a gift from God that we are not free to end on our own terms."*

Physician-Assisted Suicide Is Unethical

Peter J. Bernardi

In the following viewpoint, Peter J. Bernardi maintains that physician-assisted suicide is an unethical and dangerous practice that should not be approved or legalized. Bernardi opposes the actions of Jack Kevorkian, who has assisted numerous patients in suicide. Bernardi, a Catholic priest, is a doctoral candidate in systematic theology at Catholic University of America in Washington, D.C.

As you read, consider the following questions:

1. How does the author use the issue of abortion to illustrate the slippery slope argument?
2. What social problems does Bernardi cite to show that modern society is declining ethically?
3. What kind of future does Bernardi predict if euthanasia is legalized?

Peter J. Bernardi, "Coming Soon: Your Neighborhood T.S.C.," *America*, April 30, 1994. Reprinted by permission of the author.

Jack Kevorkian, M.D., aka "Dr. Death," pleads his case to legalize doctor-assisted suicide in front of a Sunday congregation at St. Paul's Presbyterian Church in Livonia, Mich. He is kicking off a ballot drive for a state constitutional amendment to secure this "right." The packed audience includes friends and relatives of most of the 20 people he has helped commit suicide since 1990 as well as the national executive director of the Hemlock Society, dedicated to suicide rights. The host pastor is an avid supporter. Dr. Kevorkian implacably asserts what he sees as the bottom line: "the right not to have to suffer." "This is really a right that already exists, and we already have, but which we have to put in writing because of human irrationality. Every reasonable adult is going to have to realize that if he votes 'no' on this, he is throwing his right away."

Kevorkian's simple logic resembles the glare of a single unshaded light bulb hanging in a bare cell. The cell contains a solitary inmate in pain who wants to end it all. Once again, the complex texture of human life has been deceptively and insidiously reduced to the unthinking slogan, "right to choose."

A Growing Movement

Where have we heard this "reasoning" before? Derek Humphry, longtime activist for "suicide rights" and author of the bestseller *Final Exit* (a how-to manual), was asked in an interview why the euthanasia movement had picked up momentum in recent years. (Since 1990, two referenda that would have legalized euthanasia were defeated in California and Washington by rather slim margins. Currently, euthanasia initiatives are also under consideration in Connecticut, New Hampshire and Oregon. [Ed. note: The Oregon initiative passed in November 1994 and faced immediate court challenges.])

He responded that *Roe v. Wade* was the turning point. Even Derek Humphry, the high priest of suicide, notes the connection between the legal victory of abortion rights and the growing demand for suicide rights. For when the "right to choose" to kill unborn babies was enshrined in law, founded on the "right to privacy," the suicide rights movement got new energy and legitimacy. A database search has turned up at least 34 termination-of-treatment cases that cite *Roe v. Wade*. The Circuit Court of Michigan in *Michigan v. Kevorkian* ruled that Michigan's statutory ban on assisted suicide was unconstitutionally overbroad because it interfered with the right to commit a "rational" suicide. The court relies heavily on *Roe*—which means there is a "slippery slope" leading from abortion rights to suicide rights.

"Slippery slope" is a moral argument used to oppose an action on the grounds that a principle is being conceded that has pernicious extensions and applications, perhaps not envisaged by its original proponents. Ideas and practices have logical consequences. Thus, while the "slippery slope" argument can be misused, it is surely inaccurate to call it, as an *America* article did, the "worst moral argument."

The experience of legalized abortion offers a striking case study of a slippery slope. Once the privacy principle was so legally enshrined in *Roe* as to allow the taking of innocent human life, it has become increasingly difficult, if not impossible, to brake the descent. A momentum has been established whereby the former presumption in favor of human life has given way to myriad forms of rationalizing and excusing the taking of life. Who would have dreamt in 1973 that by 1993 abortions would increase to 1.6 million annually? Very few of these abortions have to do with "hard" cases of pregnancy as a result of rape or incest or of threat to the mother's life. Most abortions are now motivated by lifestyle reasons.

The suicide rights lobby is trying to push us farther down the slope. Once again the "hard" cases are trumpeted to attract sympathy and the "right to choose" rhetoric is invoked as reason for legalization. Huge numbers of abortions have resulted from the *Roe* decision, and it can hardly be alarmist to envision similar consequences if assisted suicide is legally based on the "right to choose." Just as most abortions now are no longer "hard case" but "convenience" abortions, so will the circle of candidates for assisted suicide inevitably increase.

Indeed, Dr. Kevorkian has given candid and chilling indication of his desire to extend "suicide rights." In an address to the National Press Club in Washington, D.C., Oct. 27, 1992, he asserted that "every disease that shortens life no matter how much is terminal." Who, then, are his potential "clients"? According to him, terminal cancer patients with but six months to live comprise only 10 percent of the people who "need" assisted-suicide. This larger needy group, in his estimation, includes quadriplegics, people with M.S. and sufferers from severe arthritis!

Poor Social Climate

A realistic assessment of our society suggests a multiplicity of cultural factors that will only accelerate the slide down this slippery slope. For one, there is widespread violence that blunts our sensitivity to the value of human life. Whether it is Gen. Colin Powell's remark during the Persian Gulf War that the Iraqi soldiers would be crushed like roaches or the fact of 1.6 million unborn babies being butchered in abortion mills, the same message is propagated: Human life can be objectified and snuffed out if killing offers an advantage to the national or individual interest. When it is an encumbrance, there is little or no presumption in favor of human life.

Then there is our societal lack of patience. Change the technology—for example, increasingly speedy computers—and we "raise" our expectations. Waiting a few extra milliseconds becomes a burden. It is not a social climate that encourages the patient bearing of ills.

The fragmentation of the family and the scattering of the extended family contribute to the epidemic of lifeless loneliness. For too many people, human relationships that once might have reminded them that they are worth more than their social utility have eroded. Assisted suicide offers an attractive "solution" for avoiding the burdens and loneliness of old age. Suicide studies indicate that single, elderly white men have proportionately the highest rate of suicide. In contrast, elderly black women have the lowest rate. Is religious faith a factor here?

People Want Help, Not Death

That serial killer Jack Kevorkian hasn't been tried for murder—or at least manslaughter—and probably won't be speaks volumes about the confused, unsettled state of American mores.

Suicide is increasing alarmingly. But most people who attempt to take their own lives, and many who succeed, really don't want to die. Their acts are a desperate cry for help. Kevorkian and his ilk, who prey on troubled people and push them over the brink, are worse than those ghouls who encourage a person on the ledge of a building to jump.

Malcolm S. Forbes Jr., *Forbes*, August 2, 1993.

And we are a society that prizes being in control, being in the driver's seat. Is not doctor-assisted suicide the ultimate of illusory control whereby one is master of one's destiny? Then death and the dying process are viewed mechanically: something to master, not a mysterious reality to submit to.

But the hidden foundation under the moral platform of the suicide-rights activists is the unexamined attitude that suffering is a complete evil. As a society we find any sort of suffering increasingly difficult to bear. But the greatest works of literature, like Sophocles' *Oedipus Rex* and Shakespeare's *King Lear*, teach us that suffering affords the possibility of unimagined human growth, that growth in love and wisdom are potential fruits of suffering. Who has not been inspired and enriched by real-life stories of people courageously and patiently bearing pain and suffering, faithful to a destiny that eludes our capacity to fathom it?

The film *Shadowlands* offers an example of the humanizing impact of heroism in the face of suffering and inevitable death. The story is based on the true-life love relationship between Oxford don C. S. Lewis and an American woman named Joy Gresham. They come to share a depth of love that only the opacity of suffering and death, courageously faced without trying to control the outcome, could bring about. There is even an intense beauty to the dying process for those who have eyes to see. Philip Land, S.J., remarked not long before his death at age 82 in January 1994: "Have you noticed how much beauty goes into dying?"

On the other hand, it is not surprising to learn that, when Dr. Kevorkian was asked in a newspaper interview in the *Oakland [Mich.] Press* (Oakland County is where he has "staged" his assisted suicides) what he thought happened after death, he responded tersely: "You rot."

Are there any moral landmarks to brake our descent? With the "right to privacy" enshrined by *Roe* and the cost-containment mentality that has come to dominate health care in our society, there is not going to be much help coming from the legal and medical business fields. Indeed, the Catholic Church is the most effective moral force against this legalized self-killing movement. Catholic moral teaching maintains the legitimacy of the distinction between "positive" euthanasia (taking deliberate action that directly results in death) and "negative" euthanasia (allowing nature to take its course by not introducing any extraordinary means to maintain life). It should be no surprise that Dr. Kevorkian rejected this distinction as well as the Hippocratic Oath in the *Oakland Press* interview. He darkly predicts that some religious groups will "spare no expense" to defeat his Michigan "mercy" amendment. The opposition of the Catholic Church to the "right to suicide" is depicted as religious zealotry trying to impose its view of what is right.

A Future with Assisted Suicide

Ultimately, the religious conviction that life is a gift from God that we are not free to end on our own terms is the most effective motive for remaining opposed to doctor-assisted self-killing. But what effect would that argument have on someone who is not religious or who does not believe in God?

It is possible, however, to argue against doctor-assisted suicide without using religious arguments. Reflective people not moved by faith ought to consider the "slippery slope" experience of abortion before they assent to Kevorkian's logic. Words Edmund Burke wrote in 1790 deserve their reflection: "The effect of liberty to individuals is, that they may do what they please: We ought to see what it will please them to do, before we risk congratulations, which may be soon turned into complaints."

If assisted suicide is legalized, then, in the not too distant future, clinics are going to open up in rather nondescript "professional" services buildings. Perhaps they will be adjacent to abortion clinics. In front of these clinics, orange-vested escorts with sympathetic faces will protectively shepherd their clients to the front door, keeping them at arm's length from those "anti-choice fanatics" who would question their "right to choose." That is, suicide on demand, available in a clinically professional atmosphere where staff in reassuring white uniforms are dedicated to your "choice not to suffer." One thing is certain: These staff persons won't have to deal with unsatisfied customers suffering from post-suicide trauma.

There will be the media campaign aided by linguistic censors to insure that religious "zealots" do not impose their moral categories. Euphemisms will be coined to eviscerate the moral content of assisted suicide. Humphry's euphemism "final exit" will not catch on. It conjures up the unfortunate "final solution." How about "termination-of-suffering" clinics, T.S.C.'s for short?

The suicide rights lobby will keep the spotlight on liberation from unbearable suffering and on the right to choose. The secular media, claiming dedication to free speech, will suppress accurate information about the astounding breakthroughs in pain management and will largely ignore programs like Hospice that offer support for the terminally ill.

The T.S.C.'s will network with nursing homes and organ-donor businesses. Indeed, Kevorkian favors an "auction" for the buying and selling of human organs. He considers the donation of organs one of the "positives" of assisted suicide.

Our society is indeed on a slippery slope. The "right to privacy" is law and the "right to choose" is the slogan of the era. Morality has been made captive to such legality, and Dr. Kevorkian has a wide and sympathetic following. The culture of death bids fair to extend its domain.

Periodical Bibliography

The following articles have been selected to supplement the diverse views presented in this chapter.

Daniel Avila
"Saying No to Life: Reflections on Death and Justice," *Issues in Law & Medicine*, Winter 1993. Available from Box 1586, Terre Haute, IN 47808-1586.

Burke Balch and Randall O'Bannon
"Why We Shouldn't Legalize Assisting Suicide," *National Right to Life News*, Part I: September 14, 1993; Part II, September 20, 1993; Part III, November 5, 1993. Available from 419 Seventh St. NW, Suite 500, Washington, DC 20004.

Robert Barry
"The Paradoxes of 'Rational' Suicide," *Society*, July/August 1992.

Vicki Brower
"The Ethics of Suicide: The Right to Die May Be the Wrong Choice," *Utne Reader*, July/August 1994.

J.A. Burgess
"The Great Slippery-Slope Argument," *Journal of Medical Ethics*, September 1993.

Ronald M. Dworkin
"Life Is Sacred. That's the Easy Part," *The New York Times Magazine*, May 16, 1993.

Issues
"The Debate of Tomorrow, Today," March/April 1993. Available from *SSM* Health Care System, 477 N. Lindberg Blvd., St. Louis, MO 63141

Yale Kamisar
"'Right to Die'—Good Slogan, Fuzzy Thinking," *First Things*, December 1993. Available from 156 Fifth Ave., Suite 400, New York, NY 10010.

Gilbert Meilaender
"Human Equality and Assistance in Suicide," *Second Opinion*, April 1994. Available from 211 E. Ontario, Suite 800, Chicago, IL 60611.

Wesley J. Smith
"Better Dead Than Fed?" *National Review*, June 27, 1994.

St. Anthony Messenger
"Assisted Suicide Is Not the Answer," October 1993. Available from 1615 Republic St., Cincinnati, OH 45210.

Thomas Szasz
"Death by Prescription," *Reason*, April 1993.

Brian Young
"The Sanctity of Life," *The World & I*, April 1994. Available from 2850 New York Ave. NE, Washington, DC 20002.

2^{CHAPTER}

Should Euthanasia
Be Legalized?

Euthanasia

Chapter Preface

In recent years the voters of several states have considered propositions that would legalize assisted suicide. Oregon voters approved a measure in their state. Propositions in Washington and California, however, failed. In all three elections, the votes were close. The propositions elicited heated debates and much soul-searching on the part of the electorate.

One issue voters disagreed on was how and if legalized suicide would be regulated. Opponents feared that legalizing assisted suicide would be tantamount to legalizing murder, especially murder of the ill, elderly, and disabled. As the periodical *America* editorialized, "There is real danger of murders being committed under cover of the claim to be assisting a suicide. . . . There is a sinister likelihood that vocal minorities will soon clamor for the legalization of involuntary euthanasia—for killing old people or the severely disabled or the terminally ill."

Proponents respond to such fears by pointing out that the propositions were filled with safeguards that would protect patients from premature, unwanted death. For example, the Oregon law requires that (1) the patient have less than six months to live; (2) that a second doctor agree with the diagnosis; (3) that the patient make the request twice verbally, then once in writing; and (4) that the patient take the final step of ingesting the lethal prescription. These safeguards will be effective, proponents such as physician George Meyer believe. Meyer concludes that assisted suicide "is one of the most fundamental rights that a human being has—to decide if he or she wants to die."

Prior to the 1992 vote in California, more than 60 percent of voters favored legalized assisted suicide. But the proposition failed by a measure of 54 to 46 percent. The following chapter explores this seeming contradiction and presents debates that support and oppose legalizing euthanasia.

"As a public policy, killing cannot serve the
common good."

Legalizing Euthanasia Would Harm Society

Charles J. Dougherty

Legalizing euthanasia would cause society to devalue all life, but
especially the lives of the dying, the disabled, and the elderly,
Charles J. Dougherty writes in the following viewpoint. While
at first euthanasia might be an option, he contends, the ill
would soon feel obligated to commit suicide and physicians
would feel obligated to assist. Dougherty believes these developments would harm individuals, the health care system, and the
common good of society. Dougherty is director of the Creighton
University Center for Health Policy and Ethics in Omaha,
Nebraska, and a professor of philosophy, medicine, pharmacol-
ogy, dentistry, and nursing.

As you read, consider the following questions:

1. On what basis does the author argue that opposition to
   euthanasia is an obvious candidate for the role of the first
   premise of ethics?
2. How does the soaring cost of health care affect the
   euthanasia debate, in Dougherty's opinion?
3. How might legalized euthanasia affect physicians, according
   to the author?

Excerpted from Charles J. Dougherty, "The Common Good, Terminal Illness, and
Euthanasia." Reprinted by permission of the publisher, from *Issues in Law & Medicine*, vol.
9, no. 2, Fall 1993. Copyright ©1993 by the National Legal Center for the Medically
Dependent & Disabled, Inc.

The character of dying and how the dying are cared for has changed in profound ways in the last several decades. In all of our prior history, death for those who reached adulthood came generally in what is now midlife. It came swiftly, "a thief in the night." It came without significant resistance from medicine; little could be done to ward off impending death. Now death is generally an event of old age. It typically follows a long pattern of chronic illness and decline. It comes only after exhaustive medical interventions, some of which plainly increase the length and intensity of suffering and all of which increase costs to the health care system.

This change in dying, and especially its impact on the deaths of individuals, has produced a social consensus over the last two generations on a patient's or proxy's right to refuse life-sustaining medical measures, a hospice movement designed to improve the quality of life in dying, and a growing debate over legalization of doctor-assisted suicide and active euthanasia. What are the social dimensions of these developments, especially the third, since it stands before us as a social choice? Aside from real and projected impacts on individuals, how does our treatment of the terminally ill affect society as a whole? How might changes in social arrangements surrounding dying affect the common good? . . .

The Common Good and Killing the Dying

Most of those who oppose legalization of doctor-assisted suicide and active voluntary euthanasia ground their argument explicitly or implicitly in a simple deontic foundation: It is wrong to directly intend the death of an innocent human being, including oneself. If it is wrong to kill directly, it is wrong to assist in direct killing, even in the voluntary suicide of a terminally ill patient. For most opponents of euthanasia, these claims have a self-evidence difficult to articulate without throwing into question the very fundamentals of morality. They involve a deep respect for the mystery or sanctity of human life. They entail a commitment to a metaphysical acceptance of fate or of God's will. They express a conviction that it overreaches the human estate to seek to control destiny in such an ultimate fashion.

If these assertions seem too prosaic for such a weighty ethical issue, it is useful to recall the metaethical insight of the intuitionist tradition from Aristotle to the twentieth century Oxford philosophers. On this account, not everything in ethics can be argued for completely or fully justified on the grounds of reason. There cannot be a reason for every ethical conviction and a reason for that reason and so on, since this would initiate an invidious infinite regress. Instead, there must be some ethical first premises, some moral data, that are simply seen or given in experience. What more obvious candidate for the role of first premise in ethics than a commitment to human life that refuses to accept the directly intended killing of innocent human beings?

But concern for the common good can prescind from this important but difficult element of the debate. A common good perspective must focus on social realities and questions of the public interest. In that light, the following considerations constitute the main elements of the common good argument against legalizing the killing or assisting in the killing of the dying. These are not new arguments, but they are at the heart of the public policy debate.

Killing Would Become the Easiest Choice

First, consider the political and cultural difficulties that stand in the way of [making] . . . dying more dignified, humane, and cost-worthy. Now add a new reality: widely available and socially acceptable killing of terminally ill patients. Why bother with raising taxes for insuring appropriate hospice care for all? Why increase research dollars to develop more effective pain management? Why struggle to improve practice protocols, advance directives, medical orders, and the long-term care system? In short, why take the more difficult road to make the dying process more humane when there is social shortcut that terminates the dying process itself?

Society's Moral Fabric

As eminent bioethicist Thomas Beauchamp of Georgetown University has written, rules against killing "are not isolated moral principles," but "pieces of a web of rules" that forms a moral code. "The more threads one removes," warns Beauchamp, "the weaker the fabric becomes." For that reason, I think that the legalization of active euthanasia will have much greater impact than is generally realized on our society and on the dynamics of the sick room.

Yale Kamisar, *ABA Journal*, April 1993.

This is a serious matter of public policy in the political and economic sense, that is, a matter of sapping the will to invest in the resources necessary to improve the care of dying patients. This surely would happen were assisted suicide and euthanasia to become widely used. Proponents often claim or intimate that recourse to killing would be rare even under the most permissible laws, but there is no good reason to suppose that this would be so. A change in law would change private practice and public expectations. This, in turn, would change our collective moral psychology, making what was previously prohibited more and more socially acceptable, even expected. No doubt it will be part of the future agenda of many of those who favor legalization to remove whatever social stigma may attach to killing the dying so that it is not only permissible but often the right or obligatory thing to do. Our therapy-oriented culture would not want anyone to feel guilty for assisting in or practicing euthanasia. Thus acceptance and recourse to euthanasia would likely grow over time. The first generation after legalization might still feel some powerful moral sentiments against killing in this context; they were raised to think so. This might tend to hold the numbers down at first. But three or four generations later, Americans might come to see this as the way to die. Certainly nothing in the proponents' case for legalization is inconsistent with this future.

New Coercions

Financial pressures may also lead to incentives for active killing by limiting funding for terminal care. Legislators considering the cost of terminal care in the Medicare and Medicaid programs, or private insurers representing premium payers, may well take it as an obligation to encourage a more cost-effective way of dying. Nearly all observers agree that cost pressures will force future adoption of practice protocols based on patient condition, likely outcome, and cost of alternative treatments. If legal and widely acceptable euthanasia is added to this economic pressure, it is hard to imagine a future without practice protocols, a package of basic benefits, reimbursement restrictions, or cost-sharing arrangements that provide de facto incentives for the active killing of terminally ill patients. If this future should come to pass, the freedom to choose that many proponents of legalization champion will set the stage for not-so-subtle financial coercions that will determine how many of us die, especially the poor and uninsured or underinsured.

The general point that the will to improve dying will be compromised if active killing is legalized is relevant not only to public policy in the broad sense, but also to the social relationships that will be affected by legalized euthanasia. Why should an adult child struggle to support and care for a declining parent when such a facile alternative exists? And why should an aging parent continue to struggle—in fact, how can he or she justify what may come to be seen as the selfishness of continuing to struggle—when others do the "right thing" by their children by having themselves killed? In short, legalization will seriously erode efforts to humanize the dying process and will create its own new coercions. The hard work needed to humanize dying will simply become less and less worth it at the national and familial levels.

It might be said in response that this argument presumes that legalized killing would create new ethical realities but that contemporary medical practice has already sanctioned direct killing in the guise of the removal of ventilators and feeding tubes. There are philosophers aplenty prepared to argue that there is no longer a tenable distinction between allowing to die and direct killing. Although there are serious intellectual challenges here and contemporary medical practice has certainly entered a difficult gray zone, the distinction still has merit. The facts of dawn and dusk do not erase the distinction between night and day. There is still at the heart of the matter a profoundly important distinction in moral intention. This distinction is intuitively obvious to many families of dying patients, families prone to say things like: "We don't want to prolong Grandpa's suffering, but we cannot kill him."

Cure, Not Care

Replacement of efforts to make dying more humane with a practice of killing the dying also has a broad cultural significance. It is plainly part of the common good that we should seek moral balance in our public practices, social relationships, and institutions. Virtue or moral excellence lies between excess and deficiency; extremes should be avoided. But there is one extreme in our health care system that has been decried by ethicists and social critics throughout the late twentieth century, namely, fixation on cure to the detriment of care. Euthanasia is the apotheosis of this tendency. Instead of enhancing care for the dying patient, the condition is cured by killing the patient. Legalization will exacerbate this excess and move the health care system further away from balance and moral excellence.

A second common good consideration that counts against legalization of doctor-assisted suicide and euthanasia is the slippery slope concern. There are two moral arguments central to the proponents' case. First is the humanitarian or beneficence-based argument that a doctor-assisted or -caused death will reduce human suffering. There may be cases where the pain experienced in the dying process is simply intractable, though this is a contended claim in the debate. Suffering, of course, is inherently part of the dying process. It can be reduced by care measures typically part of hospice—psychosocial support, maximum family involvement, and spiritual counseling. But suffering in dying can only be eliminated by eliminating death or the dying. It is certainly true that pain and suffering could be lessened in total if the terminally ill died earlier and more quickly. Killing could be timed to locate the optimal mix of pleasure and pain, happiness and suffering. In theory, legalization could create a world with less pain and suffering than would be the case with continued prohibition of killing.

The second argument is based on autonomy. Competent individuals should have control over their dying as a matter of self-determination. Respect for persons entails the right to be free of paternalistic interference with one's own interpretation and pursuit of the good. In short, whose life is it anyway? Competent adults ought to be free to determine when and how they will die.

Taken together, the beneficence and autonomy arguments ground the claim the terminally ill and competent persons ought to be able to choose doctor-assisted suicide or euthanasia. But note that these two arguments are easily separable. When they are separated, the conceptual slippery slope becomes clear. Development of the pain and suffering argument alone justifies involuntary euthanasia. Why should someone be left in pain and suffering simply because he is not competent to choose death for himself? In fact, isn't it discrimination against persons who are mentally disabled to restrict access to a quick and painless death to persons who are competent?

Toward Suicide on Demand

The slide from voluntary to involuntary euthanasia is not merely a theoretical possibility. At present, Dutch pediatricians are debating proposed guidelines, written by a committee of the Dutch Pediatric Association, that would immunize doctors for performing euthanasia on disabled newborns. "The proposed guidelines recommend that the attending physician decide whether to end the child's life, with approval from the parents and other physicians" [American Medical News]. The head of the committee estimated that, even without the proposed guidelines, Dutch doctors, who have the most permissive voluntary euthanasia policies in the world, give lethal injections to ten newborns a year. Plainly, legalizing lethal injections for infants would be a step down on the slippery slope from voluntary to involuntary euthanasia. If it is taken, the slide to include other suffering children and incompetent adults would be both small and that much more likely.

On the other hand, the autonomy argument has no inherent link to pain and suffering or even to terminal illness. Suffering or not, terminally ill or not, a person has a right to self-determination. When a competent adult—regardless of somatic health or illness—understands the consequences and freely chooses them, shouldn't he or she have the right to choose death? In other words, is it not insufferably paternalistic to condition the right to choose death on certification of terminal illness, on a requirement of a doctor's consent and cooperation, before an individual can exercise his or her ultimate autonomy? The slope of this argument is a slick, steep grade. At the bottom is an unqualified right to suicide on demand. . . .

Doctors as Killers

Another reason that legalization cannot serve the common good is the negative impact on the doctor-patient relationship when the role of healer becomes conflated with the role of killer. This change would adversely affect the trust the public has in the medical profession. Because of cost pressure and the demand for greater continuity of care, future relations with physicians will probably take place more and more within organized delivery networks not unlike today's HMOs. The structural arrangement responsible for the financial savings of HMOs—prepayment for a covered package of service—is the same arrangement that raises the central moral concern about HMOs, viz., the incentive they have to undertreat. If euthanasia becomes part of the doctor-patient relationship in this context, many patients will ask themselves this question: Is my doctor's advice that there is nothing left for me but euthanasia motivated by my best interest or his, by concern for my suffering or for her delivery network? And, conflicts of interest aside, there will inevitably be this worry: Is my doctor's advice that it is time for euthanasia an expression of concern for me, or of her exasperation with a condition that can't be cured, or of his desire to be done with a case that is no longer medically interesting?

The impact on doctors is worrisome too. Though it may not be so for each doctor, medicine is motivated by a deep compassion for the sick and the dying. Some doctors who advocate legalization are plainly motivated by this compassion. In their practices, they experience the inhumane effects of contemporary dying. Their hope is that some hard cases can be dealt with more humanely by doctor-assisted suicide and active euthanasia. The political agenda of legalization is fostered by the evident professional virtues of these doctors.

But the doctors who advocate legalization today developed their admirable sympathies in a medical world that inherited a clear conviction that killing patients is professionally unethical. When it did occur, it was a private matter in which doctors who believed that killing patients is wrong in general struggled with exceptional cases—and with their own consciences. What of the generations of doctors, most of them quite ordinary men and women, who would be educated after legalization? They would be socialized into a professional ethic that says killing is an acceptable thing, perhaps the right thing, certainly the expected thing. Could they develop the same degree of compassion for suffering and for the dying as doctors of the past? Isn't it more reasonable to suppose that they would increasingly think of suffering as unnecessary, of the natural process of dying as an elective choice, of those who refuse euthanasia as curiosities or fanatics? . . .

Serving All People

A point often underscored by proponents of legalization in the context of the impact on the doctor-patient relationship is the novelty of contemporary dying. Death can be delayed as never before, resulting in prolongation of pain and suffering. Patients can be locked indefinitely in states of limbo. This is certainly true. . . . But it is also true that doctors have dealt with dying patients from the beginnings of the profession and have long had at their disposal an array of poisons capable of killing their suffering patients quickly. In other words, while the character of modern dying has surely changed, the general structure of the moral problem of euthanasia is as old as the Hippocratic Oath. Its traditional prohibition has shaped the doctor-patient relationship. Legalization of killing patients would create a profound change in medicine, a change that could bring many other unforeseen and adverse social consequences for the profession and the public it serves.

The common good must be assessed carefully in the debate over legalization of doctor-assisted suicide and euthanasia. This is not just an issue of individual rights or of the difficult deaths of a few. Respect for the common good demands creation and protection of social realities that serve all persons, though they may not serve each. Persons can be best served by adopting measures that make the process of dying more humane and dignified for all of us. In essence, this means adopting a hospice-inspired strategy of accepting death when it is inevitable, providing the best human support to ease suffering, and using every reasonable measure to control pain. But dying is not made more humane and dignified by killing. That "curative" shortcut would undermine efforts of care. Moreover, accepting killing in a few hard cases would set the stage for acceptance of widespread medical killing and would seriously undermine the doctor-patient relationship. In some terribly difficult circumstances, the killing of a dying patient may serve the good of some. But as a public policy, killing cannot serve the common good.

"Physician-aided dying would be a treatment option chosen only by those who are absolutely sure of their own desires and who are acting in a truly voluntary and informed way."

Legal Safeguards Can Prevent Euthanasia from Harming Society

John A. Pridonoff

John A. Pridonoff, who holds a doctorate in psychology, is the executive director of the Hemlock Society, which supports the option of active voluntary euthanasia for the terminally ill. In the following viewpoint, Pridonoff attempts to assuage concerns that, if legalized, physician-aided dying would lack sufficient safeguards. He describes an Oregon law legalizing physician-aided dying that contains extensive safeguards. Pridonoff concludes that laws such as the Oregon legislation are needed in order to give terminally ill patients the power to end their own suffering and to control how they die.

As you read, consider the following questions:

1. What are some of the legal safeguards included in the Oregon Death with Dignity Act, according to Pridonoff?
2. Under the Oregon Death with Dignity Act, what would happen to those who try to coerce people into suicide, according to the author?
3. What need in society is satisfied by legislation such as the Oregon Death with Dignity Act, in Pridonoff's opinion?

John A. Pridonoff, "Fear of Suffering Outweighs Death," *Insight on the News*, August 29, 1994. Reprinted with permission.

Physician-assisted dying clearly has become the bioethical issue of the 1990s. Recent right-to-die ballot measures were narrowly defeated in two states. . . . Michigan, Washington and New York all currently await the outcome of major, related court cases.

Despite the publicity accorded Dr. Jack Kevorkian and the best-selling books *Final Exit* and *How We Die*, physician-aided dying has reached this level of national debate not because of the notoriety of some of its proponents, but because of the ever-increasing sophistication of high-tech medicine and the ability of the medical community to keep the human body functioning long past its "natural" point of departure, or even its owner's wishes. As with so many modern issues, the debate about physician-aided dying has arisen because we, as a culture, have learned so well how to answer the question, "Can we do this?" and have never learned how to answer so easily the question, "Should we do this?"

Medical Progress and Problems

For most of recorded history, physician-aided dying, although surely practiced, has not been an issue. Most people died of their first major illness, and life expectancies generally were short. Noted British physician and journalist Jonathan Miller estimates that not until the beginning of the 20th century did medicine do anything to prolong the average life, and it probably killed as many people as it cured.

The discovery and use of antibiotics marked the first great change in this situation, followed by the beginning of artificial life-support systems: respirators, feeding tubes, artificial nutrition, hydration and even artificial organs. With this constantly accelerating technological change, life could be prolonged, expanded and even saved—or so it seemed.

But with the new technology, as we have learned all too well in every scientific field, came new questions. For example, what do we mean when we say "life"? Do we mean the continued functioning of the body? Of the brain? Or do we mean the continued experience of the human being? And if so, does that experience have to have quality as well as quantity?

Beginning in the 1970s, groups began to form to assert the right of physician-aided dying and to challenge legal restraints to it in the courts. First came the case of Karen Ann Quinlan, kept alive artificially until her family went to court and sued for the right to terminate life support for a brain-dead patient. (Quinlan's parents won the right to remove a respirator from her bedside in 1976; she died nine years later.) Then, in 1990, the case of Nancy Cruzan established the legal right of an individual to determine whether or not he or she would want to be kept alive artificially. Following the Supreme Court decision in the Cruzan case, Congress passed the Federal Patient Self-Determination Act, which clearly established the right of every patient to reject life-sustaining treatment.

There can be little doubt that these legal confrontations came in direct response to the changing landscape of medical science. Before the advent of machinery to artificially prolong life, the Quinlan and Cruzan cases would not have been possible. But at the same time, we witnessed an unmistakable response to the ever-worsening ways in which people died. The 1980s saw a dramatic rise in the number of reported cases of euthanasia and mercy killing. Of the 519 reported cases of assisted death between 1920 and 1993, 476 occurred after 1979. By 1994, more than 91 percent of the reported cases of euthanasia and mercy killing in the past eight decades have been reported in the last 14 years. There can be no more telling statistic to indicate the fear of modern ways of dying than this. For many people, the suffering and excruciating pain of dying in America at the end of the 20th century are far, far more frightening than death itself.

There is every indication that the same response to the horrors of uncontrolled technology and modern disease has led many doctors to the conclusion that physician-aided dying is a grim necessity of our world. It is hardly a new concept or practice. According to the posthumous memoirs of Lord Dawson of Penn, the personal physician to George V, the British king's death in 1936 was helped along by a fatal dose of morphine and cocaine. Lord Dawson gave the final dosage without raising a whimper of protest within the royal family because he had been given permission to "act at any moment to halt a painful death." In the United States, a significant number of doctors have admitted to aiding terminally ill patients in dying. But these admissions come only when the doctors are assured of anonymity. In polls that do assure such anonymity, up to 20 percent of physicians have admitted to helping their patients die, either with prescriptions or injections. There is no way of knowing how many physicians have done so but will not admit it, even with the promise of protection.

Physicians Who Have Assisted in Suicide

Why is the assurance of anonymity so essential in determining the extent of current practices? Because any doctor who admits helping a patient die will face at the very least persecution and very likely prosecution. To date, very few have stepped forward to admit their involvement. The most famous of these are Kevorkian and Timothy Quill. Kevorkian, best known to the public, has been stripped of his medical license and has faced assisted-suicide and murder charges. In 1994, the jury in his first trial sent a clear message to lawmakers by refusing to find him guilty of assisted suicide despite his open admission of his actions.

Quill's case is less well-known to the public. In 1991, Quill, a well-respected Rochester, N.Y., physician, published an article in the *New England Journal of Medicine* in which he described his agonizing decision to help a terminal cancer patient by writing her a prescription for barbiturates, knowing that she would use them to end her life before her suffering became unbearable. Quill's open admission of involvement and the description of the careful procedure he followed raised the level of the debate about physician-assisted suicide. Quill was prosecuted for his admission, but a grand jury refused to indict him after hearing the details of the case.

Concurrent with all of this legal activity, groups such as Concern For Dying and the Hemlock Society U.S.A. have spent the past two decades educating the public about the scope of the problem. Thousands of people, frightened of the possibilities of being kept alive against their wishes by artificial means, or of being left helpless in a hospital bed while their wishes and their personal agony are discounted, joined these groups, signed living wills, drew up durable powers of attorney for health care, wrote letters to their newspapers, hoarded pills and spoke out for the right of an individual to control his or her own death, just as that individual has the right to control his or her own life.

Although to its proponents change has seemed uncomfortably slow, it actually has been relatively quick. By 1990, polls indicated that 65 percent of the public favored legalizing physician-aided dying. A recent Harris poll indicated that figure now has risen above 70 percent. Public education has proceeded at a very rapid pace. Education and realization have had the same effect, if less overwhelmingly, in the medical community. Most polls indicate that a slight majority of physicians now favor the legalization of physician-aided dying, even if they might choose not to take part themselves.

Scare Tactics

But opposition to physician-aided dying has been well-organized and well-financed, mostly by the Roman Catholic Church and radical-right religious organizations. In two state referendums, Washington in 1991 and California in 1992, physician-aided dying was defeated narrowly, 54 percent to 46 percent. In both cases, opinion polls showed the referendum passing handily until the last two weeks before the election, when opponents launched massive advertising campaigns. These campaigns featured emotional and often ludicrous scare tactics, including the claim that if one bill passed, a patient's foot doctor "can kill you!" As absurd as

75

these claims are to an educated audience today, they were effective enough to scare a significant percentage of the voters, and the two measures failed.

The major concerns expressed by opponents of physician-aided dying and those who are still undecided center on the issue of safeguards. The Hemlock Society has spent more than a decade developing a system of safeguards for such legal change. These safeguards are included in the Oregon Death with Dignity Act [which was passed by voters in November 1994 and was immediately challenged in court]. In our view, this act is the finest, safest piece of legislation ever proposed for physician-aided death.

The Ultimate Right

The Hemlock Society looks forward to the day when it can scrap its suicide manual. We hope patients will have access to lawful aid-in-dying from physicians, on very clearly defined terms, and with appropriate safeguards against abuse. For me and many others, the right to die in a manner of one's own choosing is the ultimate civil liberty.

Derek Humphry, *Dying with Dignity*, 1992.

The first and most important legal safeguard is the requirement that physician assistance for a terminally ill patient be absolutely voluntary. The law put forward in the initiative specifies that the patient must be an adult, must express voluntarily the desire to die and must be competent to make an "informed decision." No one could request aid in dying for another, and the request could be made only by a mentally competent adult who was a resident of the state.

A restriction to voluntary requests from the patient is absolutely essential to ensure that aid in dying never be used by anyone for a purpose other than the relief of his or her own suffering. The purpose of this legal change is to empower the patient, not the family or the physician. Only the patient can request assistance in dying.

The second safeguard restricts to whom aid in dying would be available. The Oregon bill states very specifically that the patient must be a competent adult who is terminally ill. A terminal disease is defined within the bill as one which, within reasonable medical judgment, will "produce death within six months." Additionally, the bill mandates a second opinion from another physician. These restrictions assure that physician-aided dying couldn't be chosen by anyone who was clinically depressed and suicidal, and that the disease had reached a stage from which an end was clearly foreseeable.

The third safeguard assures that the patient would have ample time to be informed of alternative treatments and to reconsider the decision to end his or her own life. To qualify for physician assistance, the patient would have to make an oral request, then wait 15 days before repeating the request to the attending physician. If the request were repeated, the physician would have to offer the patient the opportunity to rescind the request. If the patient persists, then a written request must be made, signed and dated before two witnesses, neither of whom could be an heir or a relative. This written request then would be followed by another 48-hour waiting period. The patient could rescind the request at any time.

At the end of the second waiting period, if the patient has not rescinded the request, the patient could receive a prescription from the attending physician for a lethal dosage of medication. This elaborate system of requests may seem overly taxing for a person who is suffering greatly, but it does ensure that the patient is consistent and assured that this is the proper course of action.

Coercion Would Be Illegal

If either the attending physician or the second physician consulted were to see any indication that the patient might be suffering from a psychiatric or psychological disorder, the physician would be required to refer the patient for counseling. The physicians also would be required to report any possibility of coercion by a family member or any other party to the authorities for investigation. Coercion would remain a punishable offense. And although the physician could not require it, he or she would have to ask the patient to notify next of kin of the decision. All these measures would help to assure that physician-aided dying would be a treatment option chosen only by those who are absolutely sure of their own desires and who are acting in a truly voluntary and informed way.

The Oregon Death with Dignity Act is a very carefully crafted legal document, designed to ensure that voluntary physician-assisted death is available for those terminally ill patients whose quality of life has, in their view, become so limited or whose ability to withstand intractable pain has been so taxed that they choose to suffer no longer through what has become a hopeless dying process. As such, it answers a need that has been expressed in our society very clearly over the past 20 years—the need for dying patients to have some measure of control over how they die.

"A law against assisted suicide helps the terminally ill and the elderly much more than it hurts them."

Legalizing Euthanasia Would Encourage Suicide

Edward J. Larson

Western civilization has long opposed assisted suicide because of the threat it poses to individuals and society, according to Edward J. Larson. In the following viewpoint, Larson states that assisted suicide is still dangerous and should remain illegal. Larson maintains that legalized physician-assisted suicide is especially a threat for the mentally ill, chronically ill, and elderly, who may choose to die in order to lessen the burdens they impose on society and their families. Larson concludes that the government has a right and a duty to discourage suicide. Larson is an associate professor of history and law at the University of Georgia in Athens, and author of the book *Sex, Race and Science: Eugenics in the Deep South*.

As you read, consider the following questions:

1. What did Chief Justice William Rehnquist write in the *Cruzan* decision concerning the state's role in preventing suicide, as quoted by Larson?
2. Why does the author believe it is dangerous to consider "personal autonomy" and "self-determination" when deciding the legality of assisted suicide?
3. How do laws against assisted suicide help the terminally ill and the elderly, in the author's opinion?

Edward J. Larson, "Assisted Suicide Is a Slippery Slope," *Insight on the News*, August 29, 1994. Reprinted with permission.

There is a saying among attorneys that "bad facts make bad law." This adage has always applied to arguments for legalized mercy killing. It perfectly fits the May 1994 federal district court ruling in *Compassion in Dying vs. Washington*, in which Judge Barbara Rothstein of Seattle held that certain people have a constitutional right to receive a doctor's help in committing suicide. If upheld, this unprecedented decision would undermine all state laws against assisted suicide and euthanasia. As it stands, it illustrates how focusing on a few compelling individual cases for physician-assisted suicide—which provide the "bad facts"—can produce a legal ruling that is likely to harm many more people than it helps.

In this lawsuit, three terminally ill Washington residents challenged their state's law against assisted suicide, which is similar to statutes in most American jurisdictions. Like other states, Washington does not outlaw suicide or attempted suicide. Rather, the law at issue broadly proscribes aiding or causing the suicide of another. Nothing in the statute targets physicians as actors or the elderly, terminally ill or those in pain as recipients. It protects life and discourages suicide without regard to the victim's condition. It covers confused teenagers and depressed 40-year-olds as well as the infirm.

Restrictions against assisted suicide have been the norm in Western civilization for more than 1,500 years, and have always applied in Washington state. Although the long history and widespread acceptance of a ban against assisted suicide do not necessarily prove its wisdom, they certainly suggest that such restrictions do not so intrude upon our traditionally protected personal liberty as to violate our constitutionally protected right to privacy. Better evidence for the wisdom of this age-old ban comes from its current viability. In its present form, the Washington law reflects the relatively recent influence of the Model Penal Code, which was crafted by the leading criminal law scholars of the mid-20th century.

Protecting Life

The drafters of the Model Penal Code considered the arguments in favor of decriminalizing assisted suicide, but ultimately decided to retain that traditional feature of Anglo-American criminal law. In the commentary to the code, the drafters noted that "the interests in the sanctity of life that are represented by the criminal homicide laws are threatened by one who expresses a willingness to participate in taking the life of another, even though the act may be accomplished with the consent, or at the request, of the suicide victim."

In the 30 years following the publication of the Model Penal Code, eight states passed new statutes specifically outlawing assisted suicide and eleven other states, including Washington in 1975, revised their existing statutes. In 1991, Washington voters rejected a ballot measure, sponsored by the same organization that instigated the present lawsuit, that would have amended the law so as to permit physician-assisted suicide.

Before Rothstein's decision, there was no hint in any published judicial opinion that laws against assisted suicide were unconstitutional. Indeed, contrary to the implications of her decision, the U.S. Supreme Court in its 1990 decision involving the right to die, *Cruzan vs. Director*, suggested they were constitutional. In her decision, Rothstein wrote, "In *Cruzan*, the Supreme Court considered whether a competent person has a constitutionally protected liberty interest in refusing unwanted, life-sustaining medical treatment. . . . In his majority opinion, Chief Justice William H. Rehnquist acknowledged that this principle 'may be inferred from our prior decisions.'" She added, "The question then becomes whether a constitutional distinction can be drawn between refusal or withdrawal of medical treatment which results in death, and the situation in this case involving competent, terminally ill individuals who wish to hasten death by self-administering drugs prescribed by a physician."

Rothstein failed to note that the Supreme Court all but answered this precise question on the very same page of the *Cruzan* opinion. Almost immediately following the quoted passage suggesting that patients can refuse treatment, Rehnquist added, "Moreover, the majority of states in this country have laws imposing criminal penalties on one who assists another to commit suicide. We do not think a state is required to remain neutral in the face of an informed and voluntary decision by a physically able adult to starve to death." This observation suggests that the high court would uphold a clean ban against assisted suicide, such as Washington's statute, and that there is a constitutionally meaningful distinction between a patient's right to refuse medical treatment and her demand for assistance in committing suicide.

Public-policy arguments justify this distinction. In defense of its statute before the district court, Washington raised two of these societal interests, which were twisted by the court.

Preventing Suicide

The first justification involves preventing suicide. The court wrote, "Obviously, the state has a strong, legitimate interest in deterring suicide by young people and others with a significant natural life span ahead of them. But this case is not about people for whom suicide would abruptly cut life short. Plaintiffs in this case are people suffering through the final stage of life with no hope of recovery." Yet the court struck down the law for everyone, not just the three terminally ill plaintiffs, and did not clearly indicate what narrower restriction against assisted suicide was constitutional.

Suicide is a major social concern in both Washington and the country as a whole. It now ranks among the top 10 causes of death in the United States, with more than 25,000 cases reported annually. In Washington, suicide takes more than twice as many lives annually as all infectious diseases and causes nearly as many deaths as automobile accidents. The state vigorously seeks to combat these other causes of death, and logically attempts to discourage suicide as well. . . .

Not Just the Ill

We may be fairly sure of one thing. If we legalize active euthanasia for only the "terminally ill," it will not remain limited for very long. At first, living-will statutes provided that the directive only became operative when its maker became "terminally ill." But in response to strong criticism that such a restriction unduly limited the impact of such legislation, a growing number of states have removed the limitation either by statutory amendment or case law.

Yale Kamisar, *ABA Journal*, April 1993.

Advocates of physician-assisted suicide tend to focus on cases involving the terminally ill, particularly those who are elderly. The issue is far from simple even in those most compelling cases, however. All major suicide studies confirm that, even within the over-65 age group, only a small fraction of all suicide victims are struggling with terminal illness at the time of death. Further, nearly all victims die while they have a diagnosable psychiatric illness, which typically involves treatable depression.

In this respect, University of Rochester geriatric psychiatrists Yeates Conwell and Eric Caine warn that "many doctors on the front lines, who would be responsible for implementing any policy that allowed assisted suicide, are ill equipped to assess the presence and effect of depressive illness in older patients. In the absence of that sophisticated understanding, the determination of a suicidal patient's 'rationality' can be no more than speculation, subject to the influence of personal biases about aging, old age, and the psychological effects of chronic disease."

In dismissing defense arguments that the statute properly serves to prevent suicide, Rothstein casually added, "The court has no doubt that the legislature can devise regulations which will define the appropriate boundaries of physician-assisted suicide for terminally ill individuals, and at the same time give due recognition to the important public-policy concerns regarding the prevention of suicide." Unfortunately, this is not as easy as the court suggests.

Admittedly, the distinction that Rothstein declared unconstitutional, between patients asking for physician-assisted suicide and those requesting the termination of life-sustaining treatment, is not perfect. It is a bright line indeed, however, compared to the distinction that Rothstein drew between the "terminally ill," to whom she would grant a right to have physician assistance in committing suicide, and other seriously ill people, whose rights she did not address. University of Michigan constitutional scholar Yale Kamisar notes, "Why should the nonterminal nature of a person's suffering disqualify her as a candidate for assisted suicide? If personal autonomy and the termination of suffering are the key factors fueling the right to assisted suicide, how can we exclude those with nonterminal illnesses or disabilities who might have endured greater suffering over a much longer period of time?"

The Slippery Slope

The line is difficult to draw even at this point of objectively documented physical suffering. In a 1994 case involving a severely depressed but physically healthy individual, a Dutch court ruled that psychological suffering is sufficient to satisfy the Netherlands's liberal policy on legalized mercy killing. Shouldn't that apply here too if, as Rothstein asserted, "personal autonomy" and "self-determination" are the controlling factors?

The court's decision dealt only with assisted suicide, in which the victim performs the final act. The logic of the ruling, however, applies equally to euthanasia, in which someone else performs the final act. Washington and every other state condemn active euthanasia as murder. Yet some otherwise competent, terminally ill people are physically unable to perform a final, death-causing act. If physician-assisted suicide is a constitutional right for such people, then why should they be denied a right to die when and how they choose simply because they are too sick to kill themselves? Indeed, even though the Netherlands began by allowing physician-assisted suicide, 85 percent of its mercy killings now involve euthanasia.

Similarly, how can minors be excluded? In 1994, a Florida court ruled that a mentally competent 15-year-old boy had the same right to refuse life-sustaining medical treatment as an adult. A similar result should follow on equal-protection grounds for any constitutional right to physician-assisted suicide. There is no certain end to this slippery slope.

The second public-policy justification offered by Washington in defense of its statute involved preventing undue influence, duress, abuse and mistake in the commission of physician-assisted suicide. Rothstein acknowledged that this is "unquestionably a legitimate consideration," but then dismissed it by noting that Washington law allows individuals to refuse life-sustaining medical treatment. "The potential risk of abuse and undue influence is often just as great and may be greater in certain cases for a patient who requests to be disconnected from a life-support system," she claimed. Yet this should not preclude a different result when all factors are considered.

Saving Society

Common sense supports the view that, if physician-assisted suicide is legal, freely discussed and openly practiced, then more people, especially the infirm and the elderly, will see it as a socially accepted way to save society, their family and themselves from the burdens of old age and serious illness. Further, a person diagnosed with a terminal illness might choose physician-assisted suicide not from a desire to die, but from fear of either the pain that may come at a later stage of illness or the prospect of losing control of life-sustaining treatment decisions in the event of future incompetence. Should physician-assisted suicide be condoned, a patient might accept that route without fully exploring the very real alternatives of pain management, which can be effective in nearly every case, and advance-treatment directives that can protect a person's control over life-sustaining treatment. These factors do not apply with the same force when patients simply refuse medical treatment and let nature take its course.

Proponents of physician-assisted suicide express a sincere concern for the rights and interests of the infirm. But a state legislature reasonably could conclude that, on balance, a law against assisted suicide helps the terminally ill and the elderly much more than it hurts them. It protects them from the pressures and mistakes that could lead vulnerable human beings to premature deaths. At the very least, this is a determination—a balancing of societal benefits and burdens—that is best left to the democratic process rather than to judicial fiat.

In the course of her ruling, Rothstein conceded, "Obviously the state has a strong, legitimate interest in deterring suicide by young people." She also recognized, "It is well within the legislative prerogative to enact regulations and restrictions which will ensure that undue influence from third parties plays no part in the choice of physician-assisted suicide." This is precisely what a comprehensive law against assisted suicide does. More critically, opponents of such statutes have not shown that there is any better way to accomplish these laudable social goals.

"The claim seems unwarranted that . . . legally available euthanasia . . . would cause patients to . . . 'have themselves eliminated' in order to 'spare their families' lives and pocketbooks.' "

Legalizing Euthanasia Would Not Encourage Suicide

Lawrence J. Schneiderman et al.

Lawrence J. Schneiderman is a professor in the Department of Family and Preventive Medicine and the Department of Medicine at the University of California at San Diego. He and his colleagues studied terminally ill patients to determine to what extent such patients considered their families and the cost of their health care in decisions to continue or end treatment. The authors conclude that, because many patients already consider family and cost in their decision making, legalizing euthanasia will not cause patients to feel the need to shorten their lives in order to ease their emotional and financial burden on family and friends.

As you read, consider the following questions:

1. What assumptions have many critics of euthanasia made concerning the impact of legalization upon the ill, the elderly, the disabled, and women, according to the authors?
2. Are women more or less willing than men to spend their life savings to live as long as possible, according to the authors?
3. What limitations in their study do the authors cite?

Abridged from Lawrence J. Schneiderman, Richard Kronick, Robert M. Kaplan, John P. Anderson, and Robert D. Langer, "Attitudes of Seriously Ill Patients Toward Treatment That Involves High Costs and Burdens on Others," *The Journal of Clinical Ethics*, Summer 1994; ©1994 by *The Journal of Clinical Ethics*. Reprinted with permission.

An argument that appears in almost every critique of physician-assisted suicide and euthanasia is that the availability of legally sanctioned procedures to terminate life may induce seriously ill patients to seek to shorten their lives to avoid creating costs and burdens on others. Examples of such expressions of concern from the lay and medical press are:

> If a physician's aid in dying were to become a standard part of terminal care, there is a possibility that patients might feel compelled to request it out of fear of becoming a burden to their families. The right to die could be interpreted by a vulnerable patient as the duty to die. [R.I. Misbin, *New England Journal of Medicine*]

> The second way in which involuntary euthanasia may occur is through "encouraged" euthanasia, whereby chronically ill or dying patients may be pressured to choose euthanasia to spare their families financial or emotional strain. [P.A. Singer and M. Siegler, *New England Journal of Medicine*]

> Will not some feel an obligation to have themselves "eliminated" in order that funds allocated for their terminal care might be better used by their families or, financial worries aside, in order to relieve their families of the emotional strain involved? [Leon Kass, *Commonweal*]

The elderly are often cited as being particularly vulnerable:

> If euthanasia becomes the law of the land, how long will it take before the elderly and sick begin to feel an obligation to get out of the way? When will we see the first subtle forms of coercion used on the aging and ailing family members? [J. Farah, *Los Angeles Times*]

> [A question raised is] whether the elderly might choose suicide simply to spare their family's lives and pocketbooks. [*The New York Times*]

Writers sometimes represent women as being particularly susceptible to suggestion: "Once in the position of needing care rather than being able to give it, a woman may be all too open to the idea that everyone would be better off if she were no longer a burden on others and thus all too susceptible to a suggestion of a physician-assisted death," [Alexander Capron and Vicki Michel write in *Commonweal*].

Underlying these assertions is the assumption that if active termination of life were to become socially acceptable and legal, seriously ill patients would feel compelled to take into account costs of treatment and burdens imposed on others when making decisions about care at the end of life. They would "begin to feel an obligation to get out of the way," as Farah states. This assumes that the decisions patients make today to forgo life-prolonging treatments—in the absence of available euthanasia—do not include consideration of the costs and burdens that might be imposed on family members, loved ones, and friends. We are unaware that this assumption has ever been tested empirically.

In this viewpoint, we report the responses of seriously ill patients who were asked how long they would want to live, and what percentage of their life savings they would be willing to spend, if their treatment left them totally dependent on family and friends for daily care. We carried out this study from February 1992 through July 1993, a time when physician-assisted suicide and euthanasia were not legally available and not offered as options to the patients.

Table 1

Characteristics of Population

	Patients with AIDS		Patients with Cancer	
	Number (N = 89)	%	Number (N = 61)	%
Marital Status				
Married	3	3	35	57
Unmarried	86	97	26	43
Sex				
Female	2	2	34	56
Male	87	98	27	44
Age (years)				
<40	57	64	4	7
40-49	25	28	6	10
50-64	6	7	20	33
≥65	1	1	31	51

Our purpose was to determine how long patients would want to live and what percentage of their life savings they would be willing to spend if their treatment left them totally dependent on family and friends for daily care. The study was designed to provide evidence about the degree that patients consider being a burden on others and the cost of treatment in their decisions to terminate or continue life.

Methods

The subjects were 150 patients with cancer and AIDS (acquired immunodeficiency syndrome) who were identified by their physicians as having a five-year life expectancy of no better than 50 percent (see Table 1). The patients were contacted through cancer and AIDS clinics. All patients meeting the criterion (a life expectancy of less than five years) were offered the

California Durable Power of Attorney for Health Care (which provides space for the designation of a proxy decision maker and brief instructions about treatment) and two detailed instruction supplement forms. One instruction supplement form listed specific medical treatments that patients could choose or refuse; the second form asked patients to declare how long they would want to live under various states of illness involving diminished quality of life. The patients were also asked to indicate how long they would want to live and what percentage of their financial resources they would be willing to spend if treatment left them permanently and totally dependent on others for care.

We asked the participants two questions: (1) If the outcome of treatment left you totally dependent on family or friends for daily care (with no hope of improvement), what would be the *longest* length of time you would want to live? (2) If the outcome of treatment left you totally dependent on others for care (with no hope of improvement) *and* caused you to begin to spend your life savings, what would be the *highest* percentage you would be willing to spend?

The study was approved by the institutional review board of the University of California, San Diego Medical Center (UCSD). It was conducted as part of a larger study of the effects of advance directives on healthcare. . . .

Results

Of the subjects, 132 patients (88 percent) responded to the first question and 128 (85 percent) responded to the second question. Patients with AIDS (who were younger) were significantly more likely than patients with cancer to respond to each question. . . . Almost all those who did not respond gave as a reason that they did not understand the question or did not know enough to decide.

When patients were asked how much of their life savings they would be willing to spend if they were totally dependent on others for care, more than 75 percent expressed a wish to put some limit on their expenditures. Only 23 percent of the respondents claimed they would be willing to spend their entire life savings; a larger proportion (27 percent) said that they would not wish to spend any of their life savings. On average, patients were willing to spend 43 percent of their savings. Persons with AIDS were willing to spend significantly more of their life savings than persons with cancer. Since almost all the patients with AIDS were younger than the patients with cancer, it was not possible to estimate separately the effects of disease and age on patients' responses. Among patients with cancer, neither age nor annual income was significantly related to patients' expressed willingness to spend life savings.

Among patients with cancer, females were willing to spend, on average, 22 percent more of their life savings than were males. Unmarried patients stated that they were willing to spend an average of 19 percent more of their life savings than were married patients. . . .

Of the patients responding to the possibility of being dependent upon family and friends for care, over 85 percent stated a preference for some limitation on how long they would want to live in that condition (Table 2). Only 14 percent said that they would want to live as long as possible. Nearly twice that many (28 percent) stated that they did not want to live at all under such circumstances, and 60 percent stated that they would want to live no longer than 30 days. There were no significant differences between AIDS and cancer patients on this question.

Table 2

Length of Time that Patients Would Want to Live if Treatment Left Them Totally Dependent on Family and Friends

Length of Time	Patients with AIDS		Patients with Cancer	
	Number ($N = 85$)	%	Number ($N = 47$)	%
0 days	17	20	20	43
1-30 days	32	38	10	21
31-365 days	28	33	7	15
As long as possible	8	9	10	21
Total	85	100	47	100

Among patients with cancer, a larger percentage of women than men expressed a desire to live as long as possible (27 percent compared to 14 percent), and a larger percentage of married persons than single persons expressed a desire to live as long as possible (25 percent compared to 16 percent), but these differences were not statistically significant.

Discussion

Based on the data from this study, we believe that most seriously ill patients consider the costs and burdens they might place on others in weighing decisions about their own medical treatment. Our findings are contrary to assumptions and fears expressed by opponents of socially sanctioned euthanasia and physician-assisted suicide. It appears that women are more willing to spend their life savings than men, and women want to live at least as long as men—even if they are totally dependent on family and friends for care.

We recognize the unavoidable limits to conclusions drawn at a time when euthanasia and physician-assisted suicide are illegal. Obviously, we cannot exclude the possibility that seriously ill patients might weigh costs and burdens to a greater degree in an era of legalized euthanasia and physician-assisted suicide. However, it is clear that patients will *not* suddenly begin to consider the burdens of their treatments on others, if active termination of life becomes an available option. They already do so now.

Two important limitations of this study are worth noting. First, because the responses were obtained from a written questionnaire, it is possible that the participants did not consider the questions in as much detail as they would have if they had responded verbally in interviews with their physicians. Second, we cannot discount the possibility that patients' responses to questions about treatment might be different if euthanasia and physician-assisted suicide were available options.

We recognize that our observations are open to an alternative interpretation. One could argue that, because seriously ill patients already consider the costs of treatment and being a burden on others, they are, *a fortiori*, likely to yield to pressures for physician-assisted suicide and euthanasia. On the other hand, one could argue that, if physician-assisted suicide and euthanasia were made available, patients might well feel that they had more control over end-of-life decisions. This greater sense of control might encourage seriously ill patients to gamble with risky and unpleasant life-sustaining measures, knowing that they could cut short unwelcome consequences in well-defined ways. Thus, seriously ill patients might find it easier rather than harder to resist temptations and pressures to curtail their lives prematurely.

However, it is not the purpose of this viewpoint to add to the existing overabundance of speculative claims about the advantages and disadvantages of socially sanctioned physician-assisted suicide and euthanasia. Rather, our intent is to make a small contribution of empirical data in order to evaluate the common claim that seriously ill patients will begin to feel a need or duty to shorten their lives in order to avoid placing financial and care burdens on family and friends. Our findings convince us that most seriously ill patients under certain circumstances already consider reducing burdens placed on others when contemplating their own terminal care. Therefore, in our view, the claim seems unwarranted that socially sanctioned and legally available euthanasia or physician-assisted suicide would cause patients to "begin to feel an obligation to get out of the way" or "have themselves 'eliminated'" in order to "spare their families' lives and pocketbooks."

"Everyone . . . should be solidly in favor of legalizing physician-assisted suicide."

Physician-Assisted Suicide Is a Constitutional Right

Jack Lessenberry

Jack Lessenberry, a former national editor for the *Detroit News*, has covered Jack Kevorkian's efforts to legalize physician-assisted suicide for the *New York Times*. In the following viewpoint, Lessenberry cites several U.S. Supreme Court cases that he contends support the idea that Americans have a legal right to euthanasia. The Constitution, Lessenberry argues, guarantees Americans the right to privacy and the right to make personal decisions on their own—including the right to choose suicide or physician-assisted suicide.

As you read, consider the following questions:

1. What does the author believe is the relationship between wanting less government involvement and supporting the right to euthanasia?
2. What is the "essence of America," in Lessenberry's opinion?
3. According to Kevorkian, as quoted by the author, what is the ultimate duty and responsibility of a physician?

Abridged from Jack Lessenberry, "The Virtue of Choice." This article appeared in the April 1994 issue and is reprinted with permission from *The World & I*, a publication of The Washington Times Corporation, ©1994.

No right is held more sacred, or is more carefully guarded, by the common law than the right of every individual to possession and control of his own person, free from all restraint or interference of others . . . the right to one's person may be said to be a right of complete immunity: to be let alone.

That is from the U.S. Supreme Court's opinion in a case called *Union Pacific Railway Co. v. Botsford*. And no, that wasn't the Warren Court, or even the Warren-Burger Court: This was more than a century ago, in 1891, long before anyone thought the Court might become a job shop for social legislation hammered out on the bench.

Read those words again: *The right to be let alone.*

That is what the physician-assisted suicide issue and the man who has pioneered and personalized it, Dr. Jack Kevorkian, are really all about: freedom. This is not about the "right to die." (Like it or not, we are all going to die anyway.)

What this is all about is personal autonomy. About denying that the state has any right to compel innocent, competent adults to needlessly suffer. How can anyone who wants less government interference in his life *not* also demand the right to be free of state interference in the most intimate and personal decision of all?

And how can the state in a free society prevent a physician from using his training and expertise to evaluate each case and—where medically appropriate—to provide a soft landing out of this world for anyone who voluntarily seeks it because his "life" has turned into an agonizing and unrelievable hell?

That's why everyone—especially everyone who calls himself a conservative—should be solidly in favor of legalizing physician-assisted suicide.

What if you think taking your life for any reason is always wrong, on religious or other moral grounds? That's absolutely fine—and a decision, incidentally, that would be totally accepted and respected by Dr. Kevorkian.

But that does not give you the right to prevent another competent adult from deciding what final choice to make about his own life and body. . . .

The Right to Die

What matters is simply this: Do we have a fundamental and constitutional right of self-determination? Was the esteemed Judge Benjamin Cardozo right when he wrote, in 1914, that "every human being of adult years and sound mind has a right to determine what shall be done with his own body"?

No one would deny that the state has a compelling interest in protecting life. But the evolving history of our freedoms shows, at least as compellingly, that when everything else is equal, the essence of America is contained in that wonderful and magic phrase the U.S. Supreme Court used in 1891: *the right to be let alone.*

That's why the first immigrants came here. That's why the Bill of Rights includes in the Ninth Amendment that "the enumeration in the Constitution, of certain rights, shall not be construed to deny or disparage others retained by the people."

No, the U.S. Constitution does not talk about physician-assisted suicide. Neither does it talk about the right to own a video camera. The difference between this society and totalitarian ones is that here everything not expressly denied is assumed to be permitted—not the other way around.

Most legal scholars date the modern concepts of constitutionally protected liberty and privacy rights to *Griswold v. Connecticut*, in which the Supreme Court held in 1965 that "the framers of the Constitution believed that there are additional fundamental rights, protected from governmental infringement, which exist alongside those fundamental rights specifically mentioned in the first eight constitutional amendments."

Abortion and Suicide as Rights

Eight years later, that formed the basis of one of the Court's most significant and far-reaching rulings in history: *Roe v. Wade*, in which the Court found that a woman has a constitutionally protected right to an abortion. "The Court has recognized that a right of personal privacy or guarantee of certain areas or zones of privacy, does exist under the Constitution," the Court ruled.

Geoffrey Fieger, Dr. Kevorkian's attorney, argues persuasively that if abortion is constitutionally protected, physician-assisted suicide must be. . . .

That was part of the argument he made in 1993, when he asked Richard Kaufman, chief judge of Wayne County's circuit court, to declare a recently enacted Michigan law banning physician-assisted suicide unconstitutional.

Kaufman issued a lengthy opinion that traced the growth of the common-law doctrine of informed consent, through cases in which it has been held that a rational person has the right to refuse certain forms of medical treatment and rulings that have allowed so-called passive euthanasia in which comatose or brain-dead patients, like Nancy Cruzan or Karen Ann Quinlan, have been allowed to starve or smother to death after feeding tubes or other life support systems have been withdrawn.

Finally, Kaufman concluded:

> This Court finds that when a person's quality of life is significantly impaired by a medical condition and the medical condition is unlikely to improve, and that person's decision to com-

mit suicide is a reasonable response to the condition causing the quality of life to be significantly impaired, and the decision to end one's life is freely made without undue influence, such a person has a constitutionally protected right to commit suicide.

That decision was immediately appealed. The one thing on which both supporters and opponents of physician-assisted suicide agree is that, in the end, the Supreme Court will be called on to decide the issue.

Physician-Assisted Suicide

How it should decide is clear, given the Court's previous rulings in half a dozen cases from *Griswold* to *Roe v. Wade* to *Cruzan v. Director, Missouri Department of Health,* and stretching back to *Union Pacific Railway v. Botsford.*

There are those who say, "Yes, we know. Actually, physicians do this all the time—and that's fine. But it can never be formally addressed because to do that would be to risk setting us on a 'slippery slope' that would lead to the old and the sick being pressured to opt for suicide and get it out of the way."

A Matter of Choice

Americans have a common-law and constitutional right to refuse unwanted medical treatment. This right extends to the removal of life-sustaining equipment, including the administration of artificial nutrition and hydration. This "right-to-die" should extend to aid-in-dying, or active euthanasia, for the terminally ill, at their request.

Cheryl K. Smith, *ABA Journal,* April 1993.

"Then maybe you should abolish the presidency because [Richard] Nixon was a felon," Dr. Kevorkian says. "Abuses? Yes. There has never been any human activity free from abuse. That's why you need to make this a medical specialty, have the medical profession regulate it, and train a corps of paid specialists—I call them 'obitiatrists'—who would work for a salary only. And if you want to put in the death penalty for any doctor caught abusing this, that would be just fine with me."

"You know what the ultimate duty and responsibility of a physician is? To prevent and relieve suffering. To combat disease, which means just that: *dis-ease,* an absence of well-being. What I think a doctor should do is prevent disease . . . *by any means necessary.*"

Common sense, uncommon decency, and past legal decisions make it hard to see how the courts can fail to agree.

"It is hard enough . . . to try to figure out what is morally right and humanly good, without having to contend with . . . demands of a legal and moral right to die."

Physician-Assisted Suicide Is Not a Constitutional Right

John Leo

In a May 1994 decision, a federal judge in Washington State determined that the terminally ill have a constitutionally guaranteed right to assisted suicide. In the following viewpoint, John Leo opposes this decision. He argues that if the right to die is established as a constitutional right, it logically applies not just to the terminally ill but to all citizens. This will lead to an increase in suicide, he argues, as victims of various medical conditions demand physician-assisted suicide as an equal right. Leo also fears that a right to die will create an obligation among people "to kill or help kill." Leo is a syndicated columnist and a contributing editor for *U.S. News & World Report*.

As you read, consider the following questions:

1. How does the emotional appeal of personal narratives affect people's opinions concerning euthanasia, according to Leo?
2. Why does the author have little faith in the proposed safeguards for legalized euthanasia?
3. What is the problem with "rights-talk," in Leo's opinion?

Until May 1994, the "right to die" controversy was about where the abortion controversy was when the Sherri Finkbine case hit the media in 1962.

Finkbine, a mother of four, unwittingly took thalidomide and sought an abortion to avoid bearing a deformed child. Amid great publicity, an Arizona hospital waffled, and Finkbine eventually got an abortion in Sweden.

In her book, *Decoding Abortion Rhetoric*, Celeste Michelle Condit depicts Finkbine as a powerful myth and rhetorical device for those who wanted to legalize abortion. As Condit sees it, the Finkbine narrative told a new abortion story in the language and symbols of the old antiabortion consensus: She was married, middle-class, responsible, wanted more children and refused to break the law by seeking an illegal abortion.

"Persuasive narratives," Condit writes, "always present the most extreme cases with the most noble purposes." Finkbine was "only a first move," someone who generated a compelling story. She was Chapter 1.

Who are the compelling Chapter 1 figures in the euthanasia narrative? People like Thomas Hyde, of course, the man Jack Kevorkian was in 1994 acquitted of killing through assisted suicide. The erratic Kevorkian made the strategic mistake of entering Chapter 2 by "assisting" several people who were not terminally ill, including a woman who had beaten her son at tennis the week before. But the big trial focused on the assisted suicide of a suffering, dying man with strong emotional appeal. Most of us are fearful of a long and painful death and the prospect of being kept alive for years.

The Power of Story

The Kevorkian acquittal was hardly a decisive turning point. Over the years, other mercy killers and suicide helpers have gotten off. But it's a strong indicator of the power of compelling narratives to sway jurors who should apply the law but don't. "Society is too overwhelmed by the emotional appeal of these cases to look at the big picture," said Yale Kamisar, a University of Michigan law professor. The big picture is that once the right to intervene actively and bring about death is established, there is almost no way to prevent the rest of the chapters of this book from being written.

What if Thomas Hyde had lacked the strength to pull the string that brought on Kevorkian's carbon monoxide? Well, what's the difference, let's pull it for him or give him some pills. Freelance killing of suicidal loved ones would come along quickly. Once doctors are licensed to kill, what jury will convict a spouse or other family member who dispatches a willing person?

Several proposed plans on assisted suicide include the safeguard of at least two physicians' certifying that death is less than six months away. But these are like the old plan to limit abortion to cases of rape and incest. In a rights-oriented culture, such restrictions won't last long. Soon the medical benefit of death would be extended to those in heavy pain who are not terminally ill, and equal-rights litigation would seek to extend it to comatose patients and, inevitably, AIDS and Alzheimer patients.

Reprinted by permission of Chuck Asay and Creators Syndicate.

The rhetoric of the abortion-rights movement, with its emphasis on "choice," "self-determination" and "rights," has gradually suffused the right-to-die movement. A rather stunning May 1994 federal court ruling in Washington State explicitly linked the two issues. Judge Barbara Rothstein said that a terminally ill adult has a "constitutionally guaranteed right" under the 14th Amendment to medical assistance in committing suicide.

Her decision cited the Supreme Court's 1992 reaffirmation of abortion rights in *Planned Parenthood v. Casey* and said the suffering, terminally ill person is no less deserving of protection than a pregnant woman who wishes to abort. This seems to vault our story into Chapter 6 or 7 of the death book. Suicide is no longer a crime anywhere in America, so people are always free to kill themselves, but no previous court had ever called physician-assisted suicide a right.

Everyone's Right

Having sent this boulder downhill, Judge Rothstein was careful to set a tiny twig in its path to restrain it: The state also has a right to seek the prevention of suicide by people who are not terminally ill. The problem is this: Though the judge was careful to insert the words "terminally ill" as often as possible, the logic of the decision seems to establish the right for everyone, young or old, terminal or not. Using the language of the *Casey* decision, the ruling says that "choices central to personal dignity and autonomy . . . [are] central to the liberty protected by the 14th Amendment." But if it's a basic right, how can it be denied to those who aren't terminally ill?

Judge Rothstein dismissed the slippery slope argument, even as she hurtled down the slope herself. Once again, we are trapping ourselves by an obsession with rights-talk. In principle, rights are always absolute, unconditional. As ethicist Leon Kass writes, "It is hard enough . . . to try to figure out what is morally right and humanly good, without having to contend with intransigent and absolute demands of a legal and moral right to die." Such a right would also translate into an obligation on the part of others to kill or help kill. Isn't it time to pause and rethink this?

Periodical Bibliography

The following articles have been selected to supplement the diverse views presented in this chapter.

America — "Suicide and the Law," May 28, 1994.

Sissela Bok — "Voluntary Euthanasia: Private and Public Perspectives," *Hastings Center Report*, May/June 1994.

William F. Buckley Jr. — "Suicide, Anyone?" *The Human Life Review*, Summer 1994. Available from 150 E. 35th St., New York, NY 10016.

CQ Researcher — "Death with Dignity," February 21, 1992. Available from 1414 22nd St. NW, Washington, DC 20037.

Anne Finger — "Challenging Assisted Suicide," *The Witness*, June 1994. Available from 1249 Washington Blvd., Suite 3115, Detroit, MI 48226.

Tom Flynn — "A Case for Mercy Killing," *Free Inquiry*, Summer 1993. Available from PO Box 5, Buffalo, NY 14215.

Marcel Gervais — "What Comes After Assisted Suicide and Legalized Euthanasia?" *Origins*, February 4, 1993. Available from 3211 Fourth St. NE, Washington, DC 20017.

Yale Kamisar — "Are Laws Against Assisted Suicide Unconstitutional?" *Hastings Center Report*, May/June 1993.

Katie Letcher Lyle — "A Gentle Way to Die," *Newsweek*, March 2, 1992.

Origins — "Raising the Stakes in the Euthanasia Debate," May 26, 1994.

Nancy Osgood and Susan Eisenhandler — "Gender and Assisted and Acquiescent Suicide," *Issues in Law & Medicine*, Spring 1994. Available from Box 1586, Terre Haute, IN 47808-1586.

Robert Sedler — "The Constitution and Hastening Inevitable Death," *Hastings Center Report*, September/October 1993.

Cheryl K. Smith and Yale Kamisar — "Active Euthanasia: Should It Be Legalized?" *ABA Journal*, April 1993. Available from 750 N. Lake Shore Dr., Chicago, IL 60611.

Wesley Smith — "There's No Such Thing as a Simple Suicide," *The Human Life Review*, Winter 1994.

Should Physicians Assist in Euthanasia?

Euthanasia

Chapter Preface

A terminally ill person who wishes to commit suicide is likely to first seek the advice and help of a physician. This is because physicians know what amounts of drugs are lethal and how to administer such drugs to ensure death and prevent pain. In addition, physicians know their patients and their patients' illnesses and are therefore poised to offer personalized, expert opinions about the options available to them.

But while physicians may have the expertise to help patients die comfortably, many refuse to do so. In a study of physicians in Washington state, 39 percent believed that physician-assisted suicide is never ethical. Of the 53 percent who thought assisted suicide should be legal in some situations, only 40 percent said they would be willing to assist a patient in committing suicide. This study revealed that while a majority of physicians support assisted suicide in some cases, only a minority would be willing to assist patients in suicide.

Many of those physicians who oppose assisted suicide believe it contradicts the Hippocratic oath, the traditional vow made by most physicians. The oath states that physicians should "use treatment to help the sick, . . . but never with a view to injury and wrongdoing." The American Medical Association has stated that assisted suicide violates the oath. In a 1993 release, the organization argued that "physician-assisted suicide is fundamentally inconsistent with the physician's professional role."

But to many physicians, ending the suffering of the terminally ill through assisted suicide is a compassionate act that mirrors the values set forth in the Hippocratic oath. Physician Howard Caplan argues that "it's time . . . to fight for the right to provide the ultimate assistance to patients who know their own fight to prolong life is a losing one." Renowned physician Christiaan Barnard, the first physician to perform a heart transplant, goes even further: "It is our moral duty as doctors to carry out active euthanasia."

Physicians work to save lives. Assisted suicide puts them in the position of ending lives. Is this ethical? How does it affect the patient-physician relationship and physicians' own views of their work? The authors in the following chapter address these difficult questions and debate the ethicality of physician-assisted suicide.

"Prohibition of physician-assisted suicide handcuffs doctors who want to show compassion to patients whose bodies are irreversibly falling apart."

Physicians Should Assist in Euthanasia

Timothy E. Quill

In the following viewpoint Timothy E. Quill argues that it is the physician's job to relieve suffering, and that sometimes this requires assisting terminally ill patients in suicide. The author believes that legalizing physician-assisted suicide would help patients and improve the doctor-patient relationship. Quill is associate professor of medicine and psychiatry and head of the program for biopsychosocial studies at the University of Rochester School of Medicine and Dentistry in New York. He is also known for describing in a 1991 *New England Journal of Medicine* article how he had helped a terminally ill patient commit suicide.

As you read, consider the following questions:

1. What is the problem with comfort care, in the author's opinion?
2. What is wrong with the traditional rule forbidding doctors to intentionally aid in a patient's death, according to Quill?
3. How should physicians address spiritual and emotional suffering, in Quill's opinion?

Opinion polls show that a majority of Americans want doctors to be able to help terminally ill patients suffering intolerably to end their lives. But there is no consensus on the best way to give doctors that legal authority.

State legislatures have been reluctant to address the issue. Referendums to legalize physician-assisted death were narrowly defeated in Washington State and California largely because of concern over the adequacy of safeguards.

A third strategy, which has been led by a Washington State group called Compassion in Dying, is to challenge the constitutionality of laws prohibiting physician-assisted death. Toward this end on July 20, 1994, two colleagues and I, along with three terminally ill patients, filed suit in the Federal District Court in Manhattan against New York State for violating constitutional rights.

Our suit counters a report by the New York State Task Force on Life and the Law that recommended that the state not legalize physician-assisted suicide on the grounds that the theoretical risk to vulnerable patients outweighs the benefits. The task force took up the issue in response to an article I wrote for a medical journal describing how I helped "Diane," a terminally ill leukemia patient of mine, end her life with sleeping pills.

I wonder what "Diane" would think of the task force's recommendations. What would its members have said to her or any patient who is disintegrating as a person with no prospect of relief? What the task force portrays as a tradeoff between the theoretical benefit for society and the real suffering of a few patients radically changes focus when you or someone you love is in pain.

The task force did make some positive suggestions for helping the dying. It recommended "comfort care," which puts an emphasis on human contact, relieving symptoms and enhancing the patient's quality of life, as the standard treatment for terminal patients. It said that physicians should prescribe adequate pain-relieving medicine to dying patients even if that treatment might indirectly contribute to the patient's death and that patients should have the right to refuse treatment even if it will result in death. It insisted that doctors give careful consideration to patients who ask for help in dying, for this may be a sign of depression, unrelieved pain, a family crisis or other treatable problems.

Questions That Must Be Answered

Most advocates on both sides of the right-to-die debate agree with all these principles. Yet there remain important questions that the report did not deal with satisfactorily and that we should all ask ourselves.

How should a physician respond when comfort care stops working, suffering is intolerable and a wished-for death is the only escape?

To think that all patients can be helped with more pain-relieving medication and treatment for depression is naïve. Some are forced to act on their own to end their lives rather than continue suffering. Prohibition of physician-assisted suicide handcuffs doctors who want to show compassion to patients whose bodies are irreversibly falling apart despite excellent medical care.

Mike Lane/Baltimore *Evening Sun*. Reprinted with permission.

Is "suicide" the right word to describe this process?

Although it is technically correct, the word implies a violent self-destruction, usually stemming from mental illness. We do not call it suicide when doctors help patients in unending agony who ask that their life-sustaining treatment be stopped; we call it "allowing to die." Why, then, if a suffering patient who is not on life-support chooses to end his life, does society question the motives of everyone involved, calling it "suicide," or even "killing"?

Is it possible to legally define circumstances under which physicians would be allowed to intentionally ease a patient into death?

The simplistic ethical rule that a doctor may not intentionally aid a patient's death falls apart in real clinical situations; it may inhibit doctors from prescribing sufficient pain-relieving medicine when a patient is near death, even if the patient is in agony. We *can* legislate such difficult decisions; after all, we have laws allowing physicians to take patients off life-support—an issue that is also morally and ethically complex.

Is enacting laws better than having doctors help their patients die behind closed doors (and subject themselves to legal risks)?

When secrecy abounds, a suffering patient is at the mercy of the physician's willingness to take risks. The obvious moral good of responding to patients in extreme need must be balanced against the risk that patients might be coerced to choose death prematurely. If we legalize physician-assisted suicide, we must insure that doctors do everything possible to care for the dying before helping them end their lives. If we keep the ban, we must give doctors and patients better guidance about how to respond when they face this dilemma.

If we legalize physician-assisted suicide, should we legalize voluntary active euthanasia as well?

Physician-assisted suicide entails the doctor's making the lethal means available to the patient, who then acts on his own. In voluntary active euthanasia, the doctor provides the means and carries out the final act at the patient's request. Physician-assisted suicide is less emotionally wrenching for physicians, whereas with voluntary active euthanasia there is less chance of error in the procedure. In either case, we need safeguards to insure that physician-assisted death is only the option of last resort.

Should physicians base their decisions exclusively on physical symptoms, or should psychological and spiritual suffering also be considered medically relevant?

The physical and the mental aspects of suffering are always intertwined. A person with lung cancer who has witnessed fellow patients drown in their lung secretions may be terrified about his future, and might seek reassurance that a physician would ease his death if terminal suffocation sets in. Unless doctors are allowed to consider the psychological suffering of their patients, they will be reduced to treating bodies rather than people.

The debate over physician-assisted death is a small but important part of a broader effort to give the dying better pain relief, more understanding and more choices. Most dying patients will find dignity and adequate relief through comfort care. Physician-assisted death should only be considered when all other care is ineffective.

Though relatively few patients reach this desperate state, doctors need to be able to respond to their needs. Whether created through legislatures, referendums or the courts, a public policy is needed to insure that patients will approach the final phase of life knowing there is escape should they face their worst-case scenario.

> "The trend toward mercy-killing will continue unless leaders in health care show . . . that there is an alternative more in keeping with respect for humans as spiritual beings."

Physicians Should Not Assist in Euthanasia

E. Catherine Moroney

In the following viewpoint, E. Catherine Moroney argues that legalized euthanasia would encourage the elderly and infirm to choose assisted death and would cause patients to distrust their physicians. Instead of performing euthanasia, Moroney argues, physicians should take steps to relieve the pain and suffering of the terminally ill, such as ceasing painful and useless treatments and prescribing pain medications even though they may have the secondary effect of shortening life. Moroney, a doctor of public health, is head of the Patient Health Care Committee at the Greater Victoria Hospital Society in British Columbia, Canada.

As you read, consider the following questions:

1. What three choices for death were outlined by a nationwide study conducted in the Netherlands, according to Moroney?
2. What does the author mean by a "euthanasia mentality," and how would it affect society, in her opinion?
3. How does society treat the dying, according to the author?

Abridged from E. Catherine Moroney, "Three Choices for Death," *America*, November 21, 1992. Reprinted by permission of the author.

For decades euthanasia meant mercy-killing. To most people it still does. Lately, ethicists and lobbyists for it have added qualifiers such as "direct" and "indirect" to the word "euthanasia." Nonetheless, advocates of euthanasia leave no doubt that they still mean killing. A 1991 best seller, Derek Humphry's *Final Exit*, describes in detail various means by which a patient can commit suicide.

My title ["Three Choices for Death"] refers to the three choices identified by the commission set up in the Netherlands in 1990 to do a nationwide survey of Medical Decisions at the End of Life (MDEL). These were defined as: 1) euthanasia, understood as the intentional termination of life by someone other than the person but at his or her request; 2) non-treatment decisions, and 3) alleviation of pain or symptoms with high dosage opioids, even if this might shorten life. This three-part study, which was reported in September 1991, aimed to provide a basis to consider reform of Dutch laws that technically still ban euthanasia. Specifically, it aimed to provide a positive answer to one of these questions:

- Should euthanasia as defined be decriminalized altogether?
- Should it remain a criminal act in principle but with clear rules about when not to prosecute?
- Should the present situation continue, with no new laws?

The year-long, in-depth study reported that in 38 percent of deaths, some form of MDEL was used, the incidence being as follows: euthanasia "and related MDEL"—2.9 percent; non-treatment as the most important decision—17.5 percent; alleviation of pain by opioids of such high dosage that they might have shortened the patient's life—17.5 percent.

The Pressure to Legalize Mercy Killing

Despite its limitations, the Dutch study merits attention and commendation for making a responsible effort to discover and report openly the country's nation-wide practices regarding these life and death decisions. Indeed, although euthanasia has been at the center of public debate in the Netherlands since the early 1970's, the Government that took office in 1989 decided to postpone legal revision until more reliable information was available. The study cited is an attempt to meet this need.

Meanwhile, in England, Canada and the United States, amid much misunderstanding, the pressure to legalize mercy-killing grows. In November 1991, in the United States, a referendum taken in the State of Washington defeated a proposal to decriminalize euthanasia by a margin of only 4 percent. In Canada in the same month, the Royal Commission on Health Care and Costs in the Province of British Columbia completed its work by following an excellent set of recommendations on palliative care with a call to decriminalize mercy-killing and assisted suicide. If this recommendation is followed and the Government of Canada passes such legislation, it will be the first affluent first-world nation to take the step from caring to killing.

1. Euthanasia. Society's attitudes toward dying are complex. On the one hand, there are those who are moved chiefly by compassion. On the other, there are those whose chief concern appears to be economic.

Members of the first category include those who believe they are called to ease pain and, when possible, to accompany others through life's final stages, but not to take away life, directly or by proxy. This group tends to support enhancement of palliative care, including its spiritual aspects. Another group, also moved by compassion, but with a different value system, accepts killing in order to end the dying person's distress and tends to support euthanasia rather than the relief of pain.

A Serious Responsibility

As a physician who practices "in the front lines," I have had the privilege of caring for many individuals with terminal illness. I am proud to say that each one has been handled with compassion and care, good pain relief and emotional as well as spiritual support without any assistance in shortening "their time of dying.". . .

I take seriously the responsibility entrusted in me in the tradition of Hippocrates and am appalled that physicians, for financial gain, a sense of power or the desire not to have to deal with the more difficult problems of life, would euthanise their fellow human beings.

Steven A. Wahls, *American Medical News*, July 25, 1994.

Where the overriding concern is economic, adequate palliation of the terminally ill appears a waste of resources. Within this category are advocates of mercy-killing and those who, while rejecting it in theory, grudge the expense (sometimes comparatively slight) of giving adequate relief to the suffering, especially to the old. This latter group will not take responsibility for a lethal injection forbidden by either secular or religious law, but will deny the dying person effective pain treatment. One excuse sometimes given is that such relief may "prolong the dying process." The ethical norm, long held by the Catholic Church, that states that pain relief is lawful even if it may shorten the patient's life, is turned upside down and replaced by cruelly withholding relief (for example, hydration or antibiotics) because it might prolong life.

Among the many problems associated with euthanasia are the potential sociopsychological results to be expected from its legalization. Dr. Robert G. Twycross of Churchill Hospital, Oxford, England, in his keynote address at the Sixth Annual Symposium of the International Hospice Institute, July 1990, pointed out that where a "euthanasia mentality" has developed in society, it inevitably places the elderly and infirm under pressure to opt for "assisted death." The surveys on which Dr. Twycross bases this judgment suggest that the age and status of respondents is decisive. In a sample of economics students (presumably relatively young), 90 percent supported compulsory euthanasia for unspecified groups of people "to streamline the economy," whereas 90 percent of the elderly living in sheltered accommodations or nursing homes were against euthanasia, fearing that, when no longer in command of the situation, their lives might be ended against their will.

A Distrust of Doctors

Euthanasia, be it legalized or de facto, also affects the relationship between patients and physicians. The Dutch example is instructive. Dr. Thomas Handley, registrar of the British Columbia College of Physicians and Surgeons, in an interview with a Vancouver newspaper correspondent (B.C. *Times-Colonist*, Nov. 1, 1991), declared that Dutch doctors known to help patients orchestrate their own deaths are distrusted, particularly in the light of the physicians' commitment to preserve life.

2. Withdrawal of treatment. The Dutch study dealt also with another decision regarding the end of life—withdrawal of treatment. In North America we encounter two extremes in this regard, neither of which appears to be based primarily on benefit to the patient, which should be the key to ethical decisions.

British Columbia's Royal Commission tells a harrowing tale of energetic, potentially painful and useless measures applied to a 94-year-old woman in complete collapse. When a doctor arrived and asked the professional staff, "What are you doing?" they replied, "We have no choice . . . (she) is not a 'no code' [i.e., 'do not resuscitate']." In such cases, human and medical problems are distorted into legal ones. Fear of litigation, and not patient welfare and the dictates of a sane, educated conscience, controls both the continuation of useless procedures and their withdrawal.

The other extreme entails cessation of care. This occurs when the attending physician fails to prescribe appropriate medication for pain. A gross example of this was reported in *Time* magazine in February 1988, based on an article which had appeared anonymously in the *Journal of the American Medical Association* on Jan. 8. A resident physician described how he had administered a lethal dose of morphine to a young woman in intense pain from ovarian cancer. In the controversy that followed, Minneapolis neurologist Ronald Cranford insisted that it was not the hapless resident who had been suddenly summoned to intervene in a terrible crisis, but the woman's regular physicians, who were "the real criminals." The point, I think, is that effective pain relief should be given not to end life but to ease suffering, and this must be done even if it happens that the medication has the secondary effect of shortening life, or of prolonging it in greater ease.

3. *Palliative Care.* Dr. Elizabeth Latimer, Director of Palliative Care, Hamilton Civic Hospitals, Hamilton, Ontario, writes in the *Canadian Medical Association Journal* (January 1991) that care of persons who are dying reflects the deep moral issue of how society chooses to esteem its frailest members. On the same subject, Joyce A. DeShano, Vice President of the Sisters of St. Joseph Health System, Ann Arbor, Mich., speaking from many years' experience, notes that society often alienates or separates people classified as "dying," whereas in reality there is no such group of people. Dying persons are people still living whose death is apparently more imminent than our own. Once they are put in the "dying" category, however, they are often treated without respect for their feelings and even without politeness, despite modern society's claim to be in favor of "death with dignity." But, insofar as any external force can do this, it is not tubes or respirators but callous or ill-trained attendants, turning dying people into objects, who deprive them of dignity. No matter how ravaged by disease and age, a person has intrinsic dignity. Those who fail to recognize and honor this diminish their own. . . .

Facing the Problem: Palliative/Pastoral Care

At the same symposium that Dr. Twycross attended, Dr. Derek Doyle of St. Columba's Hospice, Edinburgh, Scotland, reported that thousands of doctors and nurses recognize that there is much suffering that they could easily relieve if they had the training to match their commitment. They feel the need of specialized education in professional skills, as well as the availability of basic medications. Dr. Doyle found that where palliative medicine is recognized as a full specialty, it has achieved the standing it requires in order to attract outstanding doctors who will devote their lives to it and teach it to those in other branches of medicine.

World leaders in palliative care have long stressed the need for support and development of education and research in this field and the practical application of its results. This applies equally to pastoral care. Every person has spiritual needs—even when religious affiliation does not play a part. To meet these needs, well-qualified pastoral care givers are required. On the basis of her many years at the bedside of dying persons, Joyce A. DeShano writes: "Death is a mystic experience and the dying deserve companions. One night a patient asked me, 'How can I believe there is a God waiting for me on the other side, when there's no one waiting with me here?' You and I may be the only 'God' some people will meet. We must be there."

The trend toward mercy-killing will continue unless leaders in health care show in practice, right at the bedside, that there is an alternative more in keeping with respect for humans as spiritual beings. Progress in promoting this alternative depends on vigorous promotion of palliative/pastoral care. This calls for the united efforts of health care professionals, led by doctors and supported by church leaders and by an informed public. Through education and research, we must all understand more and do better, humbly acknowledging as we proceed that we really know little about the true nature of dying.

"Let's be honest: despite our best efforts, some deaths are simply too horrible to believe."

Physician-Assisted Euthanasia Is Necessary

Theresa M. Stephany

Theresa M. Stephany is a registered nurse who cares for patients in a hospice. In the following viewpoint, she maintains that while hospices go a long way in aiding the dying, the deaths of some patients are too horrible to be comfortable and dignified. Stephany concludes that assisted suicide should be a legal choice for such patients.

As you read, consider the following questions:

1. Stephany states that most ill patients who request suicide are not in pain. Why, then, do they seek death, in her opinion?
2. What burdens does terminal illness place on families, according to the author?
3. What is Stephany's goal concerning the legalization of assisted suicide?

Theresa M. Stephany, "Assisted Suicide: How Hospice Fails." Reprinted with permission of *The Journal of Hospice and Palliative Care*, vol. 11, no. 4, July/August 1994.

As a Labor and Delivery Nurse, I favored home births because I believed women should remain in control of their own bodies. Today, as a seasoned hospice nurse, I disagree with hospice's official position against assisted suicide because I still believe in the right to control one's body. Some people want help ending their lives and hospice fails them when it does not provide that choice.

Retaining Dignity

Make no mistake, the vast majority of my patients desperately want to live. Despite body parts that are eaten away by cancer or edema so great that swollen limbs literally weep for relief, most patients are hoping for a miracle. In my practice, a patient's request for assisted suicide, the plea of ". . . please, I've had enough," has *not* been about poor pain or symptom control. The very occasional patient who is determined to end his/her life (about one patient every two years) is *not* in pain. The patient simply prefers death to the life he or she is left with.

Also, contrary to popular sentiment, caring for a terminally ill loved one may indeed be a burden—both personally and financially—on a family. Most neighbors are not willing to assume responsibility for 24 hours/day, seven days/week care. Many extended families are logistically too far away to help. Grown children may live in distant states and cannot afford to take unpaid family leave time. Most must work full-time to keep their health care insurance and make mortgage payments. Lastly, harsh as it sounds, some families simply do not want to be caregivers. They do not relish the thought of weeks/months of bedbaths, pureed foods, and incontinence care. "If I had wanted to be a nurse, I would have become one," they tell me, and they mean it.

It is insulting to assume that patients who request assisted suicide are clinically depressed. Most are just realistic. They know what lies ahead and they'd rather not continue with it. Let's be honest: despite our best efforts, some deaths are simply too horrible to believe. We've all seen it—the toes that turn black and fall off; the cancer that eats through the patient's face, exposing jawbones and eye sockets; the blood that spurts out of friable, irradiated skin; and the inhuman secretions that ooze from head and neck cancers. Such deaths, beyond our control despite the finest symptom management, are not even remotely life-affirming. It makes me crazy when the righteous talk about how there is no need for suicide because hospice can provide a comfortable death with dignity. Is wasting syndrome, dementia, choking, diarrhea, or hemorrhage comfortable and dignified?

Hospice tries hard, but we cannot guarantee every patient a peaceful death, and we know it. If we say that we can, we are misleading our families. If we believe that hospice affirms life, we must be willing to let our patients live and end theirs as they wish. As currently practiced, hospice takes patients only so far, then releases them—alone—into the "underworld" to get the specific information they need from the Hemlock Society USA or Derek Humphry. It saddens me to develop honest, meaningful relationships with patients, then bow out when they ask for what they really want. We abandon patients just when they need us most, and the bright ones know it.

IT'S WHAT'S COME TO BE KNOWN AS RESPECT FOR THE DIGNITY OF LIFE.

PATIENT: JO
AGE: 117
CONDITION

— AND THE WORST THINGS IN LIFE AREN'T FREE.

I'd like to see hospice work with state legislators to draft humane legislation permitting assisted suicide for those who want it. I'd like to see assisted suicide be a legal *choice*, a choice for patients *and* for physicians and nurses who may or may not elect to participate. Just as all physicians/nurses do not perform abortions, all hospice personnel need not assist in deaths. Professionals who cannot do so should not be pressured; those of us who can ". . . push the plunger of the syringe" will perform that service. Choice must be available to both patients and health professionals.

Despite its rhetoric and good intentions, today's hospice care does not provide what many patients are genuinely seeking—a voice in the type of help they want.

"Vastly improved hospice training for health care professionals . . . can render the issue of euthanasia and assisted suicide essentially moot."

Physician-Assisted Euthanasia Is Unnecessary

David Cundiff

David Cundiff is an oncologist and hospice care physician in California. In the following viewpoint, Cundiff maintains that terminally ill patients do not have to resort to euthanasia to escape their pain and suffering. The hospice approach to treatment can make dying easier for the terminally ill by relieving their physical symptoms and providing them and their families with psychological and social support, according to Cundiff. Instead of legalized euthanasia to relieve the suffering of the terminally ill, Cundiff advocates increased physician training in pain management techniques and greater public education about the potential effectiveness of hospice.

As you read, consider the following questions:

1. What is the primary goal of hospice care, in Cundiff's opinion?
2. How common is it for terminally ill patients to request euthanasia, according to the author?
3. Why is pain management not offered to more patients in the United States, according to Cundiff?

Excerpted from David Cundiff, *Euthanasia Is Not the Answer*, Totowa, NJ: Humana Press, 1992. Reprinted by permission of the publisher.

The word "euthanasia" comes from a Greek phrase meaning "good death." In today's society it means killing a terminally ill person as a way to end that person's pain and suffering. Unfortunately, most people equate terminal cancer or AIDS with constant, unrelieved pain and suffering. Fortunately, today's medicine can greatly alleviate the pain and suffering from these and other diseases in all dying people. But it is also regrettably true that the majority of physicians in the United States have never been taught the techniques of treating the physical, psychological, and emotional symptoms of terminal disease. . . .

Allowing the Terminally Ill to Die Naturally

Euthanasia or "active euthanasia" is often confused with allowing the terminally ill person to die naturally of the disease. Allowing an individual to die means foregoing or stopping medical treatments intended to prolong life. For example, a terminally ill person on a respirator (breathing machine) in an intensive care ward may request that the machine be turned off and that he or she be allowed to die. The discontinuation of life support technology when any realistic hope for recovery has completely vanished is a legal, ethical, and appropriate act also known as passive euthanasia.

A poor substitute term for "allowing to die," "passive euthanasia" implies that there is a strong similarity with active euthanasia. Proponents of active euthanasia argue that the difference between passive and active euthanasia is little more than semantic. But though it is simple, the difference is much more than that. In one case, the person dies naturally of the disease process, whereas in the other, the person is killed by the injection of an overdose of medication. The US courts and medical associations also make this critical distinction.

The decision to allow a terminally ill person to die usually comes after multiple treatments have failed to cure or control a patient's disease and the prognosis is poor. Patients themselves, and family members, begin to appreciate that further heroic treatment would only prolong suffering and dying and not give a realistic chance at remission or recovery. These situations occur every day in American hospitals. . . .

Hospice or Palliative Care

The hospice approach to the treatment of the terminally ill focuses on relieving the physical symptoms of patients and on providing psychological and social support for both patient and family. Whereas standard medical treatment for cancer and AIDS patients strives to prolong life at virtually any cost, hospice seeks to optimize the quality of life of the patient's remaining time. The National Hospice Organization defines the hospice philosophy as:

Hospice affirms life. Hospice exists to provide support and care for persons in the last phases of incurable disease so that they might live as fully and comfortably as possible. Hospice recognizes dying as a normal process whether or not resulting from disease. Hospice neither hastens nor postpones death. Hospice exists in the hope and belief that, through appropriate care and the promotion of a caring community sensitive to their needs, patients and families may be free to attain a degree of mental and spiritual preparation for death that is satisfactory to them.

Palliative care is a synonym for hospice.

With notable exceptions, hospice or palliative care services in the United States are woefully inadequate. Improved training in hospice for all medical professionals and the allocation of a greater proportion of cancer and AIDS treatment resources to hospice care are urgently needed.

Who Wants Euthanasia

Informal polls among cancer specialists show that requests for euthanasia or assisted suicide are very uncommon. Two of my oncologist colleagues with more than 25 years of combined experience reported that only two of their patients had ever asked for euthanasia or assisted suicide. The published literature confirms my impression about the rarity of euthanasia requests despite the frequency of poorly treated physical and psychological symptoms.

Why do some terminally ill people want euthanasia or assisted suicide? By all accounts terminally ill people wanting euthanasia or suicide cite *pain* as the chief factor driving them to end their lives.

I have treated several thousand cancer and AIDS patients in the past 18 years, first as a medical oncologist (cancer treatment specialist), and then as a palliative care doctor. Ten of my patients have asked for euthanasia. Another fifteen or twenty attempted suicide. Only three that I know about actually succeeded in committing suicide.

In my experience the cases in which terminally ill people either requested euthanasia or committed suicide are similar. Poor pain control, other physical symptoms out of control, or inadequate psychosocial support occur invariably. Cases from the literature in which detailed information is provided confirm this impression.

Tragically, in the vast majority of these cases, the pain could have been readily alleviated and other physical symptoms suffered by these patients could have been better controlled if the caregivers had expertise in palliative care techniques. More appropriate psychological, social, and spiritual support might well have been provided if the physicians, nurses, and other health

117

care workers were adequately trained.

It is a disgrace that the majority of our health care providers lack the knowledge and the skills to treat pain and other symptoms of terminal disease properly. The absence of palliative care training for medical professionals results in suboptimal care for almost all terminally ill patients and elicits the wish to hasten their own deaths in a few. . . .

Hospice Provides Support

Hospice care is centered on the philosophy of humanistic medicine, which cares for the whole person, including the family. It aims at preparing the terminally ill person to die with dignity. . . . Studies have shown that patients in a hospice program experience less anxiety, helplessness, inadequacy, and guilt than patients who receive care in an acute-care general hospital.

George M. Burnell, *Final Choices*, 1993.

Most of the general public believes that physicians and nurses do all that is humanly possible to control pain from cancer. Few people realize that most physicians should be much better trained to treat the physical and psychological symptoms associated with terminal illness than they are. As a result, many people develop a sense of hopelessness, thinking that little can be done to relieve the pain and suffering of the dying process.

Most practicing physicians in the United States have not seen first-rate cancer pain management and the optimal control of the physical symptoms of cancer and AIDS. *They don't know that they don't know how to do it.* Unfortunately, the norm in caring for patients with end-stage disease is to expect poor pain control with poor palliative care overall. Therefore, physicians in training imagine that when the attack on cancer is stopped there is nothing else that can be done. They think that's simply the way it is when you're dying of cancer. . . .

Based on my clinical experience, information in the medical literature, and discussions with countless other doctors, I share the feeling of other specialists in hospice and pain management everywhere that most of the pain of advanced cancer and AIDS can be controlled. . . .

The Alternative to Euthanasia

The unnecessary physical and mental torment of dying in a standard medical setting can be incredible. However, with excellent palliative care, the dying process can instead be associated with profound emotional and spiritual growth for the patients, as well as for the loved ones and caregivers.

Ideally, the debate surrounding the legalization of euthanasia should center around the inadequacies of palliative care in this country, but this has not been the case. Neither the pro-euthanasia nor the anti-euthanasia forces have sufficiently highlighted the inadequacies of palliative care training or the meager medical resources directed toward hospice. Nor has either camp offered tangible proposals for alleviating the unnecessary suffering of the terminally ill.

Hospice Education

Hospice should be at the top of the agenda for health care reform in this country. Improved hospice services can simultaneously improve the quality of care and reduce its cost. Increased access to medical care services naturally follows the discovery of a low-cost, high-quality alternative therapy.

Education of the public about these issues is necessary to effect change. One hopes that the controversy so strongly stirred by the state euthanasia initiatives [in Washington in 1991 and California in 1992] will stimulate concerned citizens to learn much more about hospice. With increased public awareness, leaders in the health care field will follow. Action by American legislators, insurance companies, medical administrators, health educators, and other concerned citizens is essential if the hospice approach is to grow, and thus produce a dramatic improvement in the treatment of cancer patients.

Vastly improved hospice training for health care professionals, along with better quality and greater availability of hospice services can render the issue of euthanasia and assisted suicide essentially moot.

"Like active euthanasia, assisted suicide is never morally permissible: both are acts of intentional killing."

Physicians Might Abuse Legalized Euthanasia

Edmund D. Pellegrino

Proponents of legalized physician-assisted suicide argue that procedural guidelines and legal safeguards could prevent physicians from abusing their power to help others die. In the following viewpoint, Edmund D. Pellegrino disagrees. He contends that in determining if assisted suicide should be performed, physicians would be required to make various subjective assessments, which could lead even well-intentioned doctors to abuse their power. Physicians may also be tempted to encourage assisted suicide to relieve themselves of the frustrations, fatigue, and emotional strains of caring for a terminally ill patient, Pellegrino contends. Pellegrino is a physician affiliated with Georgetown University Medical Center in Washington, D.C.

As you read, consider the following questions:

1. Why does the author oppose euthanasia?
2. How might a physician's personal values affect his or her ability to accurately assess a patient's willingness to die, in Pellegrino's opinion?
3. How are compassion and principle related, according to the author?

Abridged from Edmund D. Pellegrino, "Compassion Needs Reason, Too," *JAMA* 270 (August 18, 1993):874-76. Copyright ©1993, American Medical Association. Reprinted by permission of the American Medical Association.

A growing number of physicians today believe that it is morally permissible, perhaps even required, to assist certain of their patients in the act of suicide. They take their inspiration from Dr. Timothy Quill's account of the way he assisted his young patient, Diane, to kill herself. They are impressed by Quill's compassion and respect for his patient. Like him, they would limit the physician's participation in suicide to extreme cases in which suffering is unrelenting, unrelievable, and unbearable. Like him, they follow a flawed line of moral reasoning in which a compassionate response to a request for assisted suicide is deemed sufficient in itself to justify an ethically indefensible act.

Quill provides a more formal and systematic outline of what he believes the appropriate response of physicians should be to a request for suicide. He emphasizes that the reasons for the request must be identified and ameliorated (ie, pain and depression should be properly treated and psychosocial and spiritual crises resolved). To do these things properly, physicians themselves must listen and learn; accept their own mortality; be compassionate, honest, and "present" to their patients; and remain "open" to assisted suicide. If this approach fails to relieve suffering, Quill deems the case extreme enough to justify transgressing the ethical proscription against assisted suicide. . . .

The most important ethical question [is] whether in certain cases assisted suicide can be ethically justified. This is the heart of a debate that is far from settled. It cannot be settled here. Elsewhere, I have tried to show that, like active euthanasia, assisted suicide is never morally permissible: both are acts of intentional killing; they are violent remedies in the name of beneficence; they seriously distort the healing purposes of medicine; they are based on erroneous notions of compassion, beneficence, and autonomy; and they divert attention from comprehensive palliative care. Moreover, euthanasia and assisted suicide are socially disastrous. They are not containable by placing legal limits on their practice. Arguments to the contrary, the "slippery slope" is an inescapable logical, psychological, historical, and empirical reality.

Making the Morally Wrong Morally Right

[The] assumption is that assisted suicide can sometimes be justified, ie, a morally wrong act can be made morally right if the process used in deciding to perform it and the way it is performed are compassionate and beneficently motivated. The moral psychology of an act has a certain weight in assessing an agent's guilt, but not in changing the nature of the act itself. Even a person's consent is insufficient to make suicide morally right. Nor is it justified by a gentle or genteel "approach" to the act. This, for example, is the stance of those who reject Jack Kevorkian's unseemly and peremptory use of his death machine, but commend Quill's modulated approach. To be sure, Kevorkian shows a shocking disregard for the most elementary responsibilities of a physician to a patient who becomes desperate enough to ask for assisted death. But regardless of whether patients use Kevorkian's machine or Quill's compassionate prescription for sedatives, they are dead by premeditated intention. In either case, physicians, who are the necessary instruments of the patient's death, are as much a moral accomplice as if they had administered the dose themselves. . . .

The Temptation to Abuse

In the name of their profession to heal, physicians have heretofore refused such a dreadful office [as euthanasia]. And well they should. The self-limiting taboo stands in place precisely because the life placed in their hands is not theirs to give and take, and the temptation to abuse our trust in this regard is all too real. (In Holland, a survey of 300 physicians showed, 40 percent had performed euthanasia without the patient's request.) "Physicians," writes the University of Chicago's Dr. Leon R. Kass, "get tired of treating patients who are hard to cure, who resist their best efforts, who are on their way down. . . . Won't it be tempting to think that death is the best 'treatment' for the little old lady 'dumped' again on the emergency room by the nearby nursing home?" And won't the already overburdened attending physician be only too likely to jump at the request for a lethal injection, misunderstanding that the desire to quit life was an "anxious plea for help, born of fear of rejection or abandonment, or made in ignorance of the available alternatives that could alleviate pain and suffering"? The trouble with this kind of choice, argues Dr. Kass, is that, in the process, we will sweep up those who think others are tired of them, or who feel that it is selfish or cowardly not to save their families emotional strain or financial distress.

Fairly described, euthanasia is an "out," not for the patient but for those who have no stomach for themselves or others in the final hour. And what honorable physician would hang a license to kill on his office wall?

America, November 7, 1992.

Ultimately, the determination of the right circumstances [for assisted suicide] is in the physician's hands. The physician controls the availability and timing of the means whereby the patient kills himself. Physicians also judge whether the patients are clinically depressed, their suffering really unbearable, and their psychological and spiritual crises resolvable. Finally, the physician's assessment determines whether the patient is in the "extreme" category that, per se, justifies suicide assistance.

The opportunities for conscious or unconscious abuse of this power are easy to obscure, even for the best-intentioned physician. Physicians' valuation of life and its meaning, the value or nonvalue of suffering, the kind of life they would find bearable, and the point at which life becomes unbearable cannot fail to influence their decisions. These values will vary widely even among those who take assisted suicide to be morally licit. The physician might . . . be honest and compassionate and listen to the patient, but find it virtually impossible to separate personal values from interaction with the patient.

Moreover, physicians must face their own frustrations, fatigue, and secret hopes for a way out of the burdens of caring for a suffering, terminally ill patient. The kind of intense emotional involvement Quill describes in Diane's case can induce emotional burnout in which the physician moves imperceptibly from awaiting the patient's decision and readiness, to subtle elicitation of a request for death. "Getting it over with" may not be only the patient's desire, but that of the physician, other health professionals, and family and friends. Each will have his or her own reason for being open to assisting in suicide. Each reason is capable of being imputed to a vulnerable, exhausted, guilty, and alienated patient. When assisted suicide is legitimated, it places the patient at immense risk from the "compassion" of others. Misdirected compassion in the face of human suffering can be as dangerous as indifference. . . .

The decision to respond to a request for assistance in suicide can be as much a danger to, as a safeguard of, the patient's right to self-determination. If it is known to be a viable option at the outset, it cannot fail to influence the patient, the physician, and everyone else involved in the patient's care. If it is not known at the outset, the patient is deprived of the clues needed to interpret her physician's actions. . . .

Compassion is a virtue, not a principle. Morally weighty as it is, compassion can become maleficent unless it is constrained by principle. In the world's history, too many injustices have been committed in the name of someone's judgment about what was compassionate for his neighbor. Compassion, too, must be subject to moral analysis, must have its reasons, and those reasons must also be cogent.

> "We recommend that physician-assisted death be legalized with adequate safeguards to protect vulnerable patients."

Safeguards Could Prevent Physicians' Abuse of Euthanasia

Franklin G. Miller et al.

In the following viewpoint, Franklin G. Miller and his associates propose safeguards that would prevent physicians from abusing their power should assisted suicide be legalized. The authors contend that physicians must have the option of helping terminally ill patients die. They argue that by regulating assisted suicide and involving ethics consultants and committees in the decision-making process, society can help physicians ease the suffering of the dying while preventing them from abusing their power. Miller is a professor at the Center of Biomedical Ethics at the University of Virginia School of Medicine in Charlottesville.

As you read, consider the following questions:

1. Why do the authors believe assisted suicide should be legalized?
2. What should be the objectives of a policy regulating assisted suicide, in the authors' opinion?
3. What are palliative-care consultants and palliative-care committees, and what would be their roles in assisted suicide, according to the authors?

Adapted from Franklin G. Miller, Timothy E. Quill, Howard Brody, John C. Fletcher, Lawrence O. Gostin, and Diane E. Meier, "Regulating Physician-Assisted Death," *The New England Journal of Medicine* 331 (July 14, 1994):119-23. Reprinted with permission. The original article contains references not reproduced here.

Public-opinion polls have consistently shown that approximately 60 percent of the American public favors legal reform allowing physician-assisted death as a last resort to end the suffering of competent patients. Yet the voters in Washington State in 1991 and California in 1992 narrowly defeated referendums that would have permitted physicians to prescribe or administer lethal treatment to terminally ill patients. The lack of adequate safeguards to protect vulnerable patients and prevent abuse may have been an important factor in the rejection of these legislative proposals. In this viewpoint we describe a policy of legalized physician-assisted death restricted to competent patients suffering from terminal illness or incurable, debilitating disease who voluntarily request to end their lives. Integral to this policy is a framework of regulation with safeguards that we believe are adequate to protect patients, preserve the professional integrity of physicians, and assure the public that voluntary physician-assisted death occurs only as a last resort. . . .

Because it exists in a legal limbo, physician-assisted suicide currently occurs in secret, without publicly sanctioned criteria and guidelines and without any independent scrutiny. A physician's willingness to assist in the death of a patient may depend as much on his or her attitude toward legal risk and authority as on the compelling nature of the patient's request. Accordingly, the legal status quo regarding physician-assisted death does not adequately serve the needs of patients with unrelievable suffering; rather, it compromises the professional integrity of physicians and undermines respect for the law. . . .

Objectives of Regulatory Policy

We believe a policy regulating physician-assisted death should be designed with the following objectives: (1) to promote comfort care as standard treatment for dying patients; (2) to permit physician-assisted death only for competent patients suffering from terminal or incurable debilitating illnesses who voluntarily and repeatedly request to die; (3) to develop and promote practice guidelines for voluntary physician-assisted death aimed at making lethal treatment available only as a last resort for unrelievable suffering; (4) to provide independent and impartial oversight of decisions to pursue voluntary physician-assisted death without undue disruption of the doctor-patient relationship; (5) to provide a mechanism for prospective committee review of difficult or disputed cases; and (6) to ensure public accountability.

Our recommended policy reflects choices concerning two difficult issues: whether physician-assisted death should be limited to physician-assisted suicide, thus excluding voluntary, active euthanasia, and whether eligible patients must be only those for whom death is imminent or whether those who are not terminally ill but who suffer from incurable and debilitating conditions such as amyotrophic lateral sclerosis may also be considered eligible. We have opted for a liberal, inclusive policy with respect to these issues. To confine legalized physician-assisted death to assisted suicide unfairly discriminates against patients with unrelievable suffering who resolve to end their lives but are physically unable to do so. The method chosen is less important than the careful assessment that precedes assisted death. Limiting physician-assisted death to patients with terminal illness would deny this option of last resort to incurably, but not terminally, ill patients who make a rational decision to end their lives because of unremitting suffering. Physician-assisted death would be appropriate only after thorough consideration of potential ways to improve the patient's quality of life. We believe that the regulatory safeguards described below would minimize the risks associated with the legalization of physician-assisted death for patients who are not terminally ill and with the possibility of voluntary, active euthanasia.

The general responsibility for regulating physician-assisted death would be lodged with regional palliative-care committees. Case-specific oversight of decisions to undertake physician-assisted death would be provided by physicians certified as palliative-care consultants, who would report to the palliative-care committees. Treating physicians would be prohibited from providing lethal treatment without prior consultation and review by an independent, certified palliative-care consultant. The palliative-care committee would be available for prospective review in difficult or disputed cases.

In order to ensure that physician-assisted death is voluntary, which is the inviolable cornerstone of this policy, only adults with decision-making capacity should be eligible for physician-assisted death. Written or witnessed oral consent by the patient must be obtained. No physician would be obligated to participate in physician-assisted death. Treating physicians would be required to report death by assisted suicide or the administration of lethal treatment to the proper public authority. Physicians who provided lethal treatment without compliance with the legal requirements would be liable to professional sanctions and criminal penalties.

Palliative-Care Consultants

Independent and impartial oversight by a certified palliative-care consultant is a vital safeguard in this proposed policy of legalized physician-assisted death. Palliative-care consultants would be physicians with experience in treating dying patients, who were knowledgeable about and committed to comfort care, skilled in the assessment of the decision-making capacity of patients suffering from terminal or incurable conditions, and well educated about the ethics of end-of-life decision making. . . .

Review by an independent palliative-care consultant would be required whenever a patient and a physician, after thorough deliberation, agreed to pursue the option of physician-assisted death. This consultative oversight would include the examination of medical records and interviews with the treating physician, the patient, and interested members of the patient's family. The consultant would review the patient's diagnosis and prognosis and explore whether the treating physician and patient had considered carefully all reasonable alternatives. The process of consultation might lead to improved pain management or the use of other means of comfort care. The consultant would assess the voluntariness of the patient's request to die and the strength of his or her resolve, paying careful attention to the possibility of distorted thinking or undue pressure by others who might be burdened with caring for the patient. The consultant could request additional expert advice if there was uncertainty about the patient's competence or medical condition or about the adequacy of palliative measures.

A Safeguarding Process

It would be unethical, I believe, for our profession to bring patients to a state of extended suffering and then abandon them there. Yet the threat to the integrity of the profession is real if euthanasia becomes standard practice. A safeguarding process involving certification and special qualification may address this threat.

Guy I. Benrubi, *The New England Journal of Medicine*, January 16, 1992.

Certified palliative-care consultants would have the authority to override agreements by patients and physicians to undertake physician-assisted death. The consultants would be required to prepare a reasoned and clearly articulated statement justifying their judgment that physician-assisted death was inappropriate. In addition, the patient and physician would have the right to appeal the consultant's judgment to the palliative-care committee. In all cases the palliative-care consultant would prepare a confidential written report that would be submitted to the palliative-care committee for retrospective monitoring. The palliative-care consultants would have the option of referring difficult or uncertain cases for prospective review to the palliative-care committees.

Regional palliative-care committees, made up of professional and lay members, would perform a variety of functions. The committees would develop, issue, and revise practice guidelines for physicians to supplement the legal requirements for physician-assisted death. For example, in order to avoid undue influence on vulnerable patients, the request for the consideration of lethal treatment must come from patients, and physicians should accede only after fully exploring the meaning of the patients' request to die and the available alternatives.

The palliative-care committees would be responsible for educating clinicians and the public about methods of comfort care (including pain management), ethical standards of informed refusal and discontinuation of life-sustaining treatment, and the option of physician-assisted death. This educational activity would cover topics such as the law, practice guidelines, and the relevant regulations; how treating physicians should respond to requests by patients for the termination of life; methods of comfort care as an alternative to physician-assisted death; and effective methods of lethal treatment. The committees would engage in routine retrospective monitoring of cases of physician-assisted death, basing their review on reports filed by the palliative-care consultants. Finally, the committees would review prospectively difficult cases referred by palliative-care consultants and appeals from patients or their primary care physicians when their negotiated requests for physician-assisted death were disapproved by the palliative-care consultants.

Balancing the Benefits and Burdens of Regulation

The process of regulation should be aimed at striking a balance between competing imperatives. On the one hand, physician-assisted death should not be an easy way out for suffering patients and their physicians. On the other hand, oversight should not be so restrictive and onerous as to deprive patients of an adequate response to intolerable suffering. . . .

The ethical norms of relieving suffering and respecting patients' rights to self-determination support the permissibility of voluntary physician-assisted death as a last resort for terminally or incurably ill patients. The availability of the extraordinary option of lethal treatment, however, must be accompanied by careful regulation to minimize the risk of abuse. We recommend that physician-assisted death be legalized with adequate safeguards to protect vulnerable patients, preserve the professional integrity of physicians, and ensure accountability to the public. The policy we have outlined would ensure independent and impartial review of decisions to provide physician-assisted death in response to unrelievable suffering, without undue disruption of the doctor-patient relationship.

7

"The power to kill on request is not one that physicians should have nor one that most want."

Physicians Must Work to Keep Euthanasia Illegal

Alexander Morgan Capron

In recent years Oregon legalized assisted suicide and California and Washington considered initiatives to legalize active euthanasia. Alexander Morgan Capron believes the strong showing in favor of these measures indicates that many people are so fearful of how the medical profession will treat them when they are very ill that they would rather be dead. Capron argues that the election results should be a warning to health care providers that unless they begin to pay more attention to the pain, suffering, and concerns of the dying, euthanasia will be legalized. Capron is Henry W. Bruce Professor of Law and Medicine at the University of Southern California in Los Angles.

As you read, consider the following questions:

1. In the California election, whites only slightly opposed euthanasia, while minorities opposed it to a great extent. Why is this so, in the author's opinion?
2. What specific changes in medicine are necessary to make euthanasia undesirable, according to Capron?
3. How might euthanasia be legalized, according to the author?

From Alexander Morgan Capron, "Even in Defeat, Proposition 161 Sounds a Warning," *Hastings Center Report*, January/February 1993. Reproduced by permission; © The Hastings Center.

Occasionally law that isn't made may be as significant as law that is. One such instance was the rejection on 3 November 1992 of Proposition 161 by a 54-46 majority of California voters. Had this initiative passed, the state would have been the first in the world since the Nazi era formally to permit physicians to perform active euthanasia. Even though defeated, the strong showing for this ballot measure—and the even stronger support it enjoyed outside the voting booth—sounds a loud alarm for health care professionals not just in California but across the country.

Proposition 161's defeat should not obscure the remarkable fact that millions of people are so fearful of how they think they'll be treated by the health care system when they're very ill that they'd rather be dead. Surveys taken in March and April 1993 showed that 75 percent of California voters favored the basic concept of physician aid-in-dying, 54 percent strongly so.

The percentage who opposed active euthanasia on moral or religious grounds stayed relatively constant from the early surveys until election day. But the ranks of those voting no swelled as the opposition coalition focused its advertising during the final weeks on what worked a year earlier to bring down a similar measure in Washington State by an identical margin: voters' fears that mistakes would be made. Among those who voted against, 43 percent told exit-pollsters that inadequate safeguards were the primary reason for their opposition.

Not surprisingly, the measure fared best among more liberal, highly educated, and younger voters. Male voters split 50-50, while females opposed 56-44; whites were only slightly opposed (52-48%), but the margin of defeat among black and Hispanic voters was 20 percent. What this suggests is that less powerful people (such as older, minority women) felt themselves more at risk from the measure, fearing that a policy of active euthanasia might be used against them because the law would provide insufficient protections for them.

Second Warning

The public has now twice given notice that something radical has to be done about the care of dying patients. Although specific aspects of the legislation proposed have caused some voters to back away from approving laws that they support in principle, a euthanasia initiative might well pass if physicians and others fail to remedy the underlying problems that propel this issue onto the public agenda.

If resources were the only problem, the health care system should be able to respond—after all, it consumes nearly one dollar in every six of our gross domestic product. Yet despite (or perhaps, because of) the system's extraordinary array of lifesaving technology, average people are so dissatisfied, so dismayed at how death occurs in this country, and so distrustful of physicians' ability or willingness to give them a "good death" that they will consider overturning thousands of years of medical ethics and societal prohibitions to legalize direct killing by physicians.

Some of those who favored Proposition 161 may have done so under the mistaken but unfortunately widespread impression that it was needed if patients are to avoid having their dying extended indefinitely by artificial means, such as respirators and tube feeding. In California and virtually every other state, patients need have no such fears, as the law protects their refusal of life-extending techniques beyond the point they judge to be of value, and allows authorized surrogates to refuse on their behalf if they become incapable of making their own decisions. Yet if some voters favored Proposition 161 to avoid an artificially extended dying, that merely shows the system has failed to educate patients about their rights, to encourage them to communicate their wishes about care at the end of life, and to reassure all concerned that respecting patients' wishes entails no risk of criminal or civil liability.

Another portion of those who favored Proposition 161 may have wanted to ensure that they would be able to assert control over their dying process even if they were not being sustained by artificial means. For instance, Betty Rollin has described how her mother displayed a great sense of relief once she was able to have at her bedside the means to take her own life. Yet this only further indicates that people feel the health care system does not really listen to patients and does not provide care and attention for their individual needs.

As though these readings of the narrow defeat of Proposition 161 aren't sufficient indictments of the care provided dying patients, it seems undeniable that many who favored the proposal—along with some of those who voted no because its safeguards were inadequate—regard the dying process in contemporary America as worse than death itself.

Medicine's Failure

This public perception is justified, given the failure of far too many medical practitioners to understand and apply modern pain management. The reason most lay people don't know that pain can be relieved in virtually every case (usually with means and doses that need not render patients unable to interact with their environment) is that many have themselves gone through illnesses or surgical recoveries without appropriate pain control or, worse yet, have seen loved ones die in unrelieved pain. Physicians, nurses, and other providers can—and must—overcome their cognitive and psychological impediments to providing adequate, patient-centered pain relief.

Equally if not more important will be overcoming the tendency of many physicians to withdraw from interaction with patients once cure no longer seems possible. Illness already creates a sense of isolation and loss of control in patients. No health care practitioner should ever say, "There's nothing more I can do," when his or her support and even mere presence—all that medicine could and did offer in most cases until the modern era of miracle drugs and high-tech surgery—would be of great value. Patients and their families who receive this final therapy of caring comfort are unlikely to see a need for active euthanasia.

Results of California Proposition 161 to Legalize Active Euthanasia (1992)

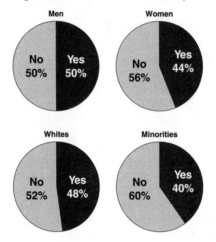

Alexander Morgan Capron, *Hastings Center Report*, January/February 1993.

Unless the health care providers who opposed Proposition 161 realize that its showing at the polls is a clear public cry for help, akin to an individual's suicide attempt, and unless they change those aspects of the system that make a quick death such an attractive alternative, support for legalizing euthanasia is sure to build and eventually to prevail. The votes in California and Washington should not be taken as encouragement for medical-practice-as-usual but as the public's wise choice to give a little more time to reform the way we care for the dying. One hopeful sign—the campaign recently launched by the state medical society in Washington to educate health care providers about care of dying patients and appropriate means of controlling pain—should inspire provider groups and medical and nursing educators across the country, without waiting for legislation or the threat of legislation elsewhere.

Both those who favor legalizing active euthanasia and those who oppose it should make it clear to their physicians and hospitals that the defeat of Proposition 161 in California may be the last warning before some state starts the ball rolling beyond education and into the law. Such a move might come fairly soon if a ballot initiative were to succeed in a smaller state such as Oregon, where the Hemlock Society now has its national headquarters. Oregon's smaller size makes a statewide campaign much less expensive and complex than in a state like California. [In November 1994, Oregon voters approved the Death With Dignity Act, legalizing physician-assisted suicide, which was immediately challenged in the courts.]

Change might also arise directly through legislation. In Michigan, where the activities of Dr. Jack Kevorkian have led to the passage of a bill that would outlaw assisting a suicide, another proposal would legalize physician-performed euthanasia. . . .

Finally, legal change could come through court decisions. If physicians and hospitals continue to do a poor job of relieving suffering and listening to their patients' wishes, judges may adopt as holdings what California Appellate Court Judge Lynn Compton expressed as dictum in his concurrence in *Bouvia*, namely, that patients have not only a right to refuse life-sustaining treatment but to command physicians' aid in ending their lives swiftly and painlessly. Although proponents of patients' rights and "the right to die" in particular have insisted for many years that withholding or withdrawing treatment is not the same as active killing, future court cases on behalf of not-quite-imminently dead patients may insist on the equivalence of the two.

So far courts that allowed the refusal of life-support have held it not to be suicide, thus also holding that cooperating physicians and nurses are not assisting suicide. The judges probably sensed the pragmatic value in maintaining distinctions that permitted physicians, nurses, and others to "have it both ways," allowing limits to be placed on medicine's ever-extending abilities to sustain biological existence while holding fast to the central cultural prohibition on killing. But legal analysts have increasingly repudiated that distinction, just as many philosophers deny any significant, intrinsic, moral difference between suicide and active voluntary euthanasia or between euthanasia and "allowing to die."

It may well be that the power to kill on request is not one that physicians should have nor one that most want, but unless they learn to take better care of dying patients, it may be a power that the public will thrust upon them.

"It should be lawful, under certain circumstances, for physicians to assist patients in ending their lives."

Physicians Must Work to Legalize Euthanasia

Frank A. Oski

Frank A. Oski is director of pediatrics at the Johns Hopkins University School of Medicine in Baltimore. In the following viewpoint, he writes that many physicians support assisted suicide as a way for physicians to ease suffering. Terminally ill patients often have no relief from pain and discomfort, he states, and physicians have the responsibility to help such patients end their lives. He concludes that assisted suicide should be legal and supported by physicians.

As you read, consider the following questions:

1. What is Oski's opinion of Jack Kevorkian?
2. Why is there so much variation between states in laws concerning assisted suicide, according to the author?
3. What guidelines does Oski suggest would help physicians who are contemplating assisting in a patient's suicide?

From Frank A. Oski, "Opting Out," *The Nation*, January 24, 1994. Reprinted with permission from *The Nation* magazine; © The Nation Company, L.P.

What we need is a brave doctor and a case which will convince the judiciary that reform is required," said British psychiatrist Colin Brewer at the sixth biennial conference of the World Federation of Right to Die Societies in 1986. We now have that brave doctor, twenty cases of physician-assisted suicide and considerable public tumult.

Dr. Jack Kevorkian should be regarded as a hero. He has taken on the tough issue that many physicians have avoided despite the pleas of anguished patients. We have legitimized advance directives, living wills and durable powers of attorney—aren't we ready for euthanasia?

Passive euthanasia is the removal of an artificial barrier to death, thus allowing nature to take its course, and is generally accepted as a humane medical practice. Active euthanasia involves affirmative action to induce death before nature can take its course in the terminally ill patient who requests it, and should be viewed as the ultimate act of humanity.

The recent debate on active euthanasia began when Kevorkian assisted in the suicide of three patients who had serious but not imminently fatal diseases. He developed a crude but effective suicide machine that allowed individuals to take their own lives in a painless and efficient fashion. After his first patient died, first-degree murder charges were brought against him but were subsequently dismissed. Kevorkian continued the practice and was jailed. He staged a hunger strike to draw public attention to the issue, and after some time in jail, and promising that further attempts at assisted suicide would not occur, he was released on bail.

A Long History for Euthanasia Supporters

The advocates of "get Kevorkian and teach him a lesson" seem ignorant of the history of the U.S. movement to legalize euthanasia, which long predates the good doctor. It began in 1906 when the Ohio legislature referred a bill to its Committee on Medical Jurisprudence, which proposed the legalization of active voluntary euthanasia. The bill was rejected by a vote of 78 to 22. Subsequent attempts to legalize the practice occurred in Nebraska, New York and recently in the state of Washington, where approximately 223,000 citizens signed a petition calling for an amendment to the state's living will law. Broad support was generated for the idea, but voters defeated Initiative 119 by a margin of 54 percent to 46 percent.

Today most states prohibit assisted suicide; Illinois, Ohio and Michigan call it murder. But even so, prosecution of those who have helped a person to die is unusual. It is not surprising that there is so much variation from state to state, because doctors themselves do not agree on the morality of active euthanasia.

135

If you become terminally ill, what can you do? Will you attempt to find a friend or physician who can help spare you the pain of a lingering death? Can physicians serve in their traditional role of healer and still assist suicides? Twelve physicians examined this issue in the *New England Journal of Medicine*. Ten of them concluded that doctors should be able to provide hopelessly ill patients who believe their condition is intolerable with the knowledge and the means to commit suicide. The group also concluded that it should be lawful, under certain circumstances, for physicians to assist patients in ending their lives.

Support for Assisted Suicide

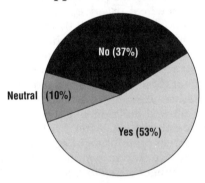

Physicians' response to the statement
"There are some situations in which
assisted suicide should be legal."

The New England Journal of Medicine, July 14, 1994.

Dr. Timothy Quill offers a more specific prescription. With several colleagues, he has proposed guidelines for physicians who find assisted suicide morally acceptable that include: 1) the patient must, of his or her own initiative, clearly and repeatedly request to die rather than continue suffering; 2) the patient's judgment must not be distorted; 3) the patient must have a condition that is incurable and associated with severe, unrelenting, intolerable suffering; 4) the physician must insure that the patient's suffering and the request are not the result of inadequate comfort care; and 5) consultation with another doctor who is experienced in comfort care should take place.

Dying patients need more than prescriptions for mind-numbing narcotics. They need a personal guide and counselor to assist them on their last journey.

Periodical Bibliography

The following articles have been selected to supplement the diverse views presented in this chapter.

Jonathan S. Cohen et al.   "Attitudes Toward Assisted Suicide and Euthanasia Among Physicians in Washington State," *The New England Journal of Medicine*, July 14, 1994.

Malcolm S. Forbes Jr.   "Why Is He Still Loose?" *Forbes*, August 2, 1993.

Issues in Law & Medicine   Entire issue on physician-assisted euthanasia and suicide, Spring 1993.

JAMA   "Decisions Near the End of Life," April 22, 1992.

Sally Johnson   "Hospital Euthanasia: Compassion or Murder?" *Insight on the News*, March 7, 1994. Available from 3600 New York Ave. NE, Washington, DC 20002.

Steven Miles   "Physicians and Their Patients' Suicides," *JAMA*, June 8, 1994.

Robert Mohan   "The Immorality and Morality of Euthanasia," *The World & I*, April 1994. Available from 2850 New York Ave. NE, Washington, DC 20002.

Timothy E. Quill   "Doctor, I Want to Die. Will You Help Me?" *JAMA*, August 18, 1993.

Betty Rollin   "The Politics of Mercy," *Family Circle*, April 26, 1994.

Robyn S. Shapiro et al.   "Willingness to Perform Euthanasia: A Survey of Physician Attitudes," *Archives of Internal Medicine*, vol. 154, no. 575, 1994. Available from 515 N. State St., Chicago, IL 60610.

Margaret Steinfels   "Euthanasia: Prospects and Perils," *Democratic Left*, January/February 1994.

Anastasia Toufexis   "Killing the Psychic Pain," *Time*, July 4, 1994.

Gerrit van der Wal   "Unrequested Termination of Life: Is It Permissible?" *Bioethics*, July 1993. Available from Basil Blackwell, 238 Main St., Suite 501, Cambridge, MA 02142.

Who Should Make Decisions About Euthanasia?

Chapter Preface

In January 1983, 25-year-old Nancy Cruzan was left permanently brain damaged as the result of a car accident. Physicians diagnosed Cruzan as being in a persistent vegetative state (PVS) and gave little or no hope of recovery. Cruzan could breathe on her own but could not perceive or interact with the outside world. She was fed through a feeding tube in her stomach.

After five years of no improvement in Cruzan's condition, her parents decided to have her feeding tube disconnected and to let her die. The hospital refused. The Cruzans then asked a Missouri trial court for permission to remove the feeding tube. The court agreed, but the Missouri Supreme Court reversed the decision, stating that only the patient herself had the right to refuse treatment, and that Cruzan had never explicitly stated before her accident that she would wish to have nutrition withheld should she ever be in a vegetative state. The U.S. Supreme Court upheld the Missouri Supreme Court's ruling, arguing that while competent adults have a right to refuse medical treatment, states also have the right to protect the rights of the incompetent.

Although they lost the appeal, the Cruzans eventually introduced new evidence to the Missouri trial court showing that their daughter had told friends she did not wish to "live like a vegetable." The court found this evidence convincing and allowed the Cruzans to force the hospital to withdraw the feeding tube. Nancy Cruzan died in December 1990.

The Cruzan case illustrates how complex and difficult it often is to determine who has the right to decide whether euthanasia should be performed on a patient. Patients alone seem to have the ultimate right to decide, but their medical conditions often leave them unable to make or communicate their own decisions. The patient's family members may understand his or her emotional suffering, but they are not objective and may make a decision that benefits them but harms the patient. The physician may have extensive knowledge about the patient's medical status but may not appreciate his or her emotional suffering. And, finally, the courts may understand a patient's civil rights but may be unaffected by the suffering of individual patients and families. The following chapter examines these issues and discusses who has the right to make decisions about euthanasia.

"Individuals have a right to determine what happens to their body."

Individuals Have the Right to Decide for Themselves

Phyllis Taylor

Individuals have the right to make decisions concerning their own bodies, including decisions about when and how to die, Phyllis Taylor writes in the following viewpoint. She argues that documents such as consent forms and living wills are necessary to allow individuals to control what happens to their bodies when they become terminally ill. Taylor, a registered nurse at Hospice of the Delaware Valley, is a co-coordinator for the ethics program at Philadelphia College of Osteopathic Medicine.

As you read, consider the following questions:

1. What examples does Taylor give of people who have been allowed to choose dignified deaths?
2. What are beneficence and non-maleficence, and how do they relate to the issue of euthanasia, in the author's opinion?
3. What fears does Taylor say make it difficult for people to face death?

Phyllis Taylor, "Dying with Dignity," *Sojourners*, August 1994. Reprinted by permission of *Sojourners* magazine, 2401 15th St. NW, Washington, DC 20009.

Mrs. S. had lived with progressive emphysema for years. During her last admission, she was brought gasping for breath into the emergency room of a local hospital. The staff asked if she wanted help breathing. She nodded her head "yes," and she was put on a respirator. Her niece arrived at the hospital hours later. She showed us her aunt's Living Will, which specified no breathing machines. We followed her wishes. She died comfortably with her niece and daughter at her side.

Contrast Mrs. S.'s situation with people who are in nursing homes, unable to converse, walk, or eat, and whose lives are maintained with feeding tubes and aggressive care when they develop pneumonia or bedsores.

We have seen the death of Jackie Kennedy Onassis, who asked to leave the hospital, stop her treatments for cancer, and stop antibiotics so she could die as she had lived, privately and with dignity. Richard Nixon had a Living Will that specified he wanted no "heroics." He, too, was allowed to die as he wished. Decorated Vietnam veteran Lew Puller and Kurt Cobain, lead singer for Nirvana, ended their lives by suicide. Dr. Jack Kevorkian gives people the means to end their lives before their diseases do. Washington State recently overturned the ban on assisted suicide. Clearly as a society we are repeatedly challenged with life-and-death issues.

I have journeyed with persons who are ill, their families, and the staffs who take care of them. And I am a religious person committed to the sanctity of life. Some of the ethical principles involved in seeking guidelines about life and living and death and dying include autonomy or self-determination, beneficence, non-maleficence, fidelity, and justice.

Benefiting the Patient

Individuals have a right to determine what happens to their body, and thus there are consent forms. As long as a person is able to communicate, he or she remains in charge of his or her body. It is part of retaining one's dignity. It is why Onassis was able to leave the hospital and to stop all treatments except those aimed at keeping her comfortable. Nixon and Mrs. S. were no longer able to express their wishes in person, but they did so through their Living Wills and durable power of attorney.

Beneficence is a principle that says medical decisions should be based on what would most benefit the patient. For example, Onassis decided that the treatments she was receiving, including antibiotics, were more burdensome than beneficial.

Non-maleficence is the duty not to harm others. Sometimes technology acts more to prolong the dying than to help with the living. At a religious conference on the question of ethics, a participant began to cry, saying that she was a devout Christian and a registered nurse and that she was having difficulty reconciling the two when she was caring for terminally ill people who were receiving very aggressive but ultimately futile care. She said that rather than feeling she was helping people, she felt she was torturing them.

Fidelity is keeping promises. We can keep our promise not to abandon the dying, but we have to couple that with the principle of justice. Part of Kevorkian's attraction is that people feel trapped in a health care system that does not listen to them or provide adequate pain and symptom management.

Why do we have so many problems recognizing that there is a time to be born but also a time to die? One reason is our fear of dying. The vast majority of people do not fear death but the dying process. They fear being in pain. The hospice movement is one way of meeting that need. We are good at managing physical pain if health practitioners use the many medications we now have available. It is unconscionable and unjust for anyone to die in pain today.

Patients' Legal Authority

Nearly all states recognize advance directives allowing patients to refuse all treatment, including food and fluids, if they are terminally ill and become permanently incompetent. Physicians are legally obligated to follow these advance directives. Thus patients have the legal authority to determine the time of their death even if they do not have the legal authority to determine the method by which they will die. Competent patients also can refuse permission for any treatment, including food and fluids, even if it is known that death will result, and even when they are not terminally ill.

Bernard Gert, James L. Bernat, and R. Peter Mogielnicki, *Hastings Center Report*, July/August 1994.

Another fear is being isolated. We are a society that denies death. This is seen in the inappropriate use of acute care hospitals, where we know that many of the sickest patients are going to die but we do everything to prevent that at the cost of great physical suffering for the patient, mental suffering for the patient, family, and caregivers, and financial expense for society. As we come to acknowledge that death is a natural part of our life as mortal human beings, we can become creative about how to address the fear of isolation.

The high cost of illness is another fear. A shifting of resources is needed, so that the emphasis is on care and comfort and not on cure in cases where a disease is progressing.

Finally, there is a fear of the unknown. Great comfort can be found in the stories of people who have had near-death experiences and those who tell us clearly or symbolically what is happening to them as they get sicker. They all talk about feeling loved. Such stories can help lessen the fear of death, if not of dying.

But what of a person who has an incurable illness such as AIDS or Alzheimer's but for whom death is not imminent? A person has the right to decide what constitutes a good quality of life. If she or he is not in crisis physically, emotionally, or spiritually and has been able to discuss all her or his fears and concerns with someone who believes in the sanctity of life, a case could be made that the person has a right to end her or his own life before the disease does. Health care providers should not be asked to assist directly, but some would say that it is valid to give the person information about medications. (Mental illness, on the other hand, is overwhelmingly painful but not incurable, and therefore seems a different situation than those involving terminal physical illnesses.)

A belief in the sanctity of life is not necessarily in conflict with a willingness to let go of this life when the body can no longer persevere without the artificial help of machines. There is a time to be born and a time to die.

> *"The family has the authority to decide when the patient cannot."*

The Family Has the Right to Decide for Loved Ones

David F. Kelly

The families of patients who can no longer make their own decisions may decide to withhold medical treatment and increase sedatives for their loved ones, even if doing so hastens death, asserts David F. Kelly in the following viewpoint. Roman Catholic faith provides guidelines for when a patient—or those making decisions for the patient—must allow or demand treatment, and for when treatment may be refused or discontinued, Kelly declares. Since such a decision is a moral one, not a medical one, he concludes, the family has both the right and the authority to make it. Kelly is a professor in the theology department of Duquesne University and hospital ethicist at the St. Francis Medical Center, both in Pittsburgh. He is the author of several books, including *Critical Care Ethics: Treatment Decisions in American Hospitals.*

As you read, consider the following questions:

1. What is the first step to take when making decisions for a dying relative, in Kelly's opinion?
2. What ethical factors limit a family's right to demand treatment for a relative, in the author's opinion?
3. What role should the cost of health care play in decisions on withholding treatment, according to Kelly?

Abridged from David F. Kelly, "If, When, and How to Die: Difficult Personal and Family Decisions," *The Catholic World*, September/October 1992. Reprinted by permission of *The Catholic World* magazine.

Most families will at one time or another face the kinds of very hard decisions which have to be made in hospitals or nursing homes about what kind of medical treatment to give to sick or dying loved ones who can no longer decide for themselves. On the one hand family members do not want to prolong uselessly the process of dying. When God calls, loving relatives are ready to let go. On the other hand, Catholic faith does not see death as a goal to be desired for its own sake, and families do want to make sure that humanly beneficial treatment is available, that procedures which offer realistic hopes for recovery are given, and that comfort measures are provided. Perhaps most important of all, families never want to abandon those whom they love, especially during the time of their dying. Yet in the presence of so many modern medical technologies, these decisions are often excruciatingly difficult. The exact line between realistic hope for human benefit and misplaced trust in medical technology that could prove useless is not always easy to find. The usually cooperative but sometimes conflictual roles of family and physician are complex psychologically, ethically, and legally. What is a family to do?

Family or Physician—Who Decides?

A few years ago I began work at St. Francis Medical Center in Pittsburgh. I started with a number of anticipations about what I would find. One of my assumptions was that most instances of conflict between physicians and families would be cases where physicians insisted on aggressive therapy while families asked to have certain medical treatments withheld or withdrawn. Physicians are trained to cure diseases through technological medicine and to ward off death whenever possible. I assumed it would be the families who would ask that their loved ones be allowed to die with dignity, free from useless technology.

But more often I found the opposite. Though the conflicts I expected do often arise, more and more today it is the families who insist on aggressive treatment while the physicians want to stop. Often physicians argue that the treatment is futile, and there has been a great deal of debate lately about what exactly is meant by "medical futility," where the physician unilaterally decides to stop treatment regardless of the family's wishes. But in our nation the right of the patient and the family to make this kind of decision is now well established. Indeed, it has been precisely the context of family desire to stop useless treatment against physician insistence on continuing that has led to this emphasis on patient and family rights in American medical ethics and in American law. So for now, with some few exceptions, families decide. What are the ethical guidelines and the ethical limits for such decisions? And does the institution or society as a whole have any ethical or legal right to refuse to treat when the family insists that everything be done?

Medical Ethics and Catholic Teaching

The first principle of importance here is the distinction, long applied by Catholic medical ethics, between "ordinary" and "extraordinary" means of treatment. Persons are obliged to take "ordinary" or "reasonable" or "proportionate" means to preserve their lives, but not "extraordinary" or "unreasonable" or "disproportionate" means. It is particularly important to note that this distinction is a moral one and not a medical one. Thus what might be a reasonable or ordinary treatment for a person who has a decent chance of recovery might well be unreasonable or extraordinary for a person whose chance of recovery is less. It is not the technical or medical characteristic of the treatment which determines whether it is "ordinary" and hence morally mandatory, or "extraordinary" and hence morally optional. For example, an otherwise healthy person who contracts pneumonia is said by the received Catholic tradition to be obliged to take antibiotics, but a person with terminal cancer need not.

The Family as a Surrogate Decision Maker

With the exception of those incompetent adults who executed advance care directives while they still were competent, incompetent individuals are unable to express their opposition to medical treatment. As a result, surrogate decision makers—usually family members or court-appointed guardians—must determine what is in incompetent individuals' "best interests."

Rosemarie Tong, *The World & I*, March 1993.

A second principle is the distinction between killing (euthanasia) and allowing-to-die. The Catholic tradition has held that to kill an innocent person, as for example in active euthanasia, is always morally wrong. But withholding or withdrawing morally extraordinary treatment is not the same as killing even if the patient dies quickly after the decision is made. Sometimes it looks like killing when a respirator or a feeding tube is withdrawn and the patient dies shortly thereafter. But Catholic teaching has consistently held that if the treatment is morally extraordinary, that is, if it is of little human benefit to the patient, or if the burdens of the treatment outweigh what human benefit there is, that treatment may be forgone. The patient dies of the disease, not of the decision to forgo the treatment. Loving families who make this kind of decision do not abandon their dying relatives and need feel no guilt about it. Rather they forgo medical treatment when it is doing no good or not enough good for the patient. Note here that there is no difference between withholding and withdrawing life-sustaining treatment. If a treatment is morally extraordinary, it may be withheld if it has not been started or withdrawn if already begun. There is no ethical or legal difference. Nor is it killing a patient when sedatives are ordered to eliminate pain even when the medication hastens the actual moment of death. The family does not intend to kill the dying patient, but rather rightly insists that enough medication be given for the patient's comfort. Even if the result is unconsciousness and a suppression of respiration which hastens the time of death, this is not considered a direct killing according to Catholic teaching. Families need feel no guilt in ordering this kind of medication.

Making the Right Decision

But these principles tell us that we *may* forgo morally extraordinary means of treatment, not that we must. Are there limits on what families may rightly request of hospitals and nursing homes? This is a very difficult issue, because it involves not only ethics, but American law as well.

In virtually all cases one can presume that the family members love their dying relative and have the patient's best interests at heart. There are probably some exceptions where hatred or revenge leads to the family's wish to be rid of a relative or to prolong the dying relative's ordeal by demanding burdensome and useless "extraordinary" treatment, but these strange situations need not concern us.

The best first step in making the right decision is to ask oneself what the dying person would have wanted. Ethically sensitive physicians and nurses, as well as hospital ethics consult teams, will ask family members this question. Often families speak about these issues. Perhaps the patient has made remarks about not wanting to be hooked up to tubes and machines which do no good, or about hoping never to be like someone on television or in the newspaper whose dying is prolonged by aggressive therapy. These simple statements are helpful guidelines to the patient's wishes. Or the patient may have filled out an advance directive, often known as a "living will." It is also possible, of course, that the sick person has stated more or less consistently that he or she would want everything done to stay alive even if it means invasive and burdensome procedures. These statements must also be considered when families make decisions. But most of us do not make such statements; most persons prefer to be allowed to die when medical technology can offer no reasonable hope for meaningful recovery.

In the absence of any evidence of the patient's wishes, even from informal conversation, family members may still decide to forgo treatment if that decision is in the best interests of the patient. Here, however, people often find themselves overwhelmed by grief, or paralyzed by denial, or ridden with guilt. I am often surprised when grieving family members insist that aggressive and almost certainly useless extraordinary treatment be continued and then state that they would never want it for themselves! Assuming that this is not an act of revenge against the dying patient, one must wonder why family members do this. I believe the reason is mainly a fear that the decision to forgo aggressive treatment will be interpreted as callousness, greed, or patient abandonment. But a proper understanding of the Catholic tradition will ease these fears. Surely if the family members who are to decide about a certain extraordinary treatment would not want it for themselves, then, unless there is clear evidence that the patient insisted on aggressive procedures in these circumstances, the treatment should be forgone.

Ethical Factors Concerning Extraordinary Treatment

Though the Catholic tradition has held that morally extraordinary treatments may be forgone, not that they must be forgone, there are, I believe, ethical factors which limit our right to demand extraordinary treatment for our dying relatives. The first of these should be quite clear. If a treatment is of no human benefit at all, or is of very little benefit, or if it offers a very slight chance of real benefit, and if at the same time it imposes significant pain or other burden on the patient, then that treatment is truly unreasonable. Loving relatives will not impose it. There is no easy way to make this calculation in theory, that is, no way to give numbers or percentages ahead of time and deduce from them a rule for right and wrong decisions. Physicians cannot be expected to give precise prognoses or exact expectations of success of various treatments. But often there does come a time when the health care team is in general agreement that further attempts are useless. If the treatment is burdensome to the patient, then the surrogate is not only ethically entitled to stop, but, I believe, ethically obliged to stop.

A second factor which enters into this context is that of cost. We have no right to throw away our precious medical resources. We are stewards of our material possessions, not absolute owners, and we have obligations to share with others. The fact that we may be tempted to spend all we can in these cases, because most often the direct costs are paid for by insurance and not by ourselves, does not change this moral obligation. Society's resources are limited.

This cannot mean that we are morally obliged to forgo clearly beneficial treatments simply because they are expensive. The problems of allocation of resources and of distributive and legal justice are far too complicated to allow any such facile rule. The Catholic tradition does hold that individuals *may* do this for themselves if they choose to; very expensive treatments, even if beneficial, do become optional on the basis of cost alone and the choice may rightly be made to forgo them even if one will die as a result, provided that the person wishes the cost to be used for a better purpose. But in the United States such decisions may not legally be made by physicians, family members or other surrogates. Thus humanly beneficial treatments may not be rejected by surrogates on the basis of cost alone.

However, though cost is not by itself sufficient to permit a surrogate to reject what would otherwise be mandatory or ordinary treatment, it is, I believe, sufficient to tip the scale when a surrogate would otherwise have an option to use or to reject morally extraordinary means of treatment. Morally extraordinary means of treatment (those with little or no benefit or those with almost no chance of benefit) may indeed become morally wrong when the cost to the common good is factored in. In the future, if our nation moves as it should toward a more just system of health care distribution and health insurance, it will be right for society to decide that its insurance will not include certain beneficial treatments which the nation simply cannot afford, given other social needs. For now, however, surrogates and physicians may not decide to reject beneficial treatment on the basis of cost.

To sum up, patients may rightly reject for themselves otherwise beneficial treatment on the basis of cost alone, if the money saved is intended for a better purpose; there is no obligation to do so, however. Surrogates may not reject otherwise beneficial treatment on the basis of cost alone. Both patients and surrogates should, however, consider cost when deciding on whether or not to use morally extraordinary (optional) treatment; such treatment may well become morally wrong if of virtually no benefit and of high cost. Finally, surrogates must reject treatment which imposes useless burdens of pain or other suffering or degradation on the patient. . . .

In almost all cases the family has the authority to decide when the patient cannot. And who is in a better position to do so? Decisions like these are moral decisions, not scientific ones, because often there is not and cannot be absolute clarity. In most instances, however, there comes a time when there is sufficient moral clarity to know that it is right to let go. The loving family recognizes that in these circumstances death is in some real way a blessing. It is time to stop the machines and let the peace of God take over.

"Public policy should provide that only mature,
mentally competent adults with acceptable
reasons are allowed to make the decision [for
euthanasia]."

Public Policy Can Guide Decisions

William McCord

William McCord (1930-1992), a sociologist at the City University
of New York, was the author of numerous books, including
Voyages to Utopia and *The Dawn of the Pacific Century*. In the following viewpoint, McCord explains his belief that euthanasia is
a decision that should be regulated by public policies. Such policies could ensure that the dying have the option of euthanasia,
he argues, and could prevent the practice from being abused by
physicians and family members.

As you read, consider the following questions:

1. What measures does the author believe would prevent
   legalized euthanasia from leading to experiments in eugenics?
2. How would McCord prevent the mentally ill from using
   legalized euthanasia as a means of suicide?
3. What will happen if no public policy concerning euthanasia
   is created, in the author's opinion?

Excerpted from William McCord, "Death with Dignity," *The Humanist*, January/February
1993. Reprinted by permission of The American Humanist Association, ©1993.

Albert Camus wrote in *The Myth of Sisyphus:* "There is only one truly important philosophic problem, and that is suicide." The significance of that sentiment—forcing each of us to a heightened awareness of the elements of human dignity, the sanctity of life, and the very meaning of existence—has perhaps never been more explicit than it is today. For the first time in history, Americans have been asked to decide the crucial question: is it morally permissible (or even admirable) for a human being to end his or her own life or to assist another in shedding this "mortal coil"?

The development of medical technology, pregnant with blessings as well as threats to keep us alive as comatose lumps of flesh, has launched this controversy, commonly labeled as issues of the "right to life." Although a quietly perennial issue, the debate became a public matter in 1974 with the landmark case of Karen Ann Quinlan, a patient whose parents requested the removal of life-sustaining machines. By 1991, 28 states had ruled that patients have the right to refuse life-sustaining treatment. In some locales, the courts indicated merely that competent, mentally alert people could make this judgment; in other states, doctors and relatives are allowed to initiate death when patients cannot request it themselves.

Nine states specifically allow the withdrawal of artificial feeding from patients in a vegetative state, allowing them to starve to death. By 1991, a federal law required that every patient admitted to any hospital for any reason must be asked if they want to plan for their death by filling out a "living will."

Medical "ethicists" have tried to draw a very fine line between withdrawing or withholding treatment and actively assisting others to commit suicide. In practice, this distinction has increasingly lost its meaning. What in fact is the difference between a doctor who starves his patient to death and one who prescribes a dose of seconal with the warning that imbibing a gram will result in death? Most reasonable people today recognize that pulling the plug on a machine or injecting a lethal dose of morphine are both "active" measures that have the same result. What remains in doubt today is who—if anyone—has the right to decide on ending life and what—if any—conditions should limit that decision.

Conflicting Opinions

These ambiguities have resulted in a quagmire of contradictory legal opinions. Some states still carry laws on their books punishing the act of suicide as a "crime"; others are silent on the issue; and some punish those who assist in a suicide as "murderers." In Michigan, for example, the State Supreme Court in 1920 upheld the murder conviction of a man who placed poison within reach of his wife, who was dying from multiple sclerosis (*People* v. *Campbell*). Yet, 63 years later, in a case that never went to trial, a Michigan appellate court ignored this precedent and dismissed a murder charge against a man who gave a gun to a person who was talking of committing suicide and subsequently killed himself.

Dr. Jack Kevorkian exacerbated Michigan's confusion in 1990 when he connected Janet Adkins, a woman suffering from Alzheimer's disease, to a suicide device and watched as she pushed the button. He took the action out of concern for the patient and a desire to force the legal and medical establishments to consider euthanasia as an ethical action. Adkins and her family, anticipating years of degeneration from the disease, requested the procedure. Dr. Kevorkian reported himself to the police immediately after she died. On July 21, 1992, murder charges against Kevorkian were finally dismissed in a Pontiac, Michigan, court; in the meantime, Kevorkian had assisted in several additional suicides.

An Action Society Should Condone

The questions of suicide and assisted suicide are before the American people in a way we cannot escape. Dr. Jack Kevorkian has assisted a number of people in taking their own lives. Always he followed certain principles. The person must be terminally ill, must be in sufficient mental or physical pain, must ask for assistance in dying properly, and must take the final act him or herself.

Why is this not an ethical action which society can condone, if not applaud?

John M. Swomley, *The Human Quest*, May/June 1994.

Voters in the state of Washington decided to put the matter on a democratic ballot. In 1991, citizens of Washington considered a legislative proposition unlike any other ever debated by Americans. Initiative 119 asked: "Shall adult patients who are in a medically terminal condition be permitted to request and receive from a physician aid-in-dying?" The proposition provided that adults could execute a medical directive requesting aid-in-dying only after two physicians certified that they were mentally competent, terminally ill, and had less than six months to live. Two independent witnesses had to certify the patient's decision.

Although public opinion polls indicated that 61 percent of Washingtonians favored the initiative, a majority of voters—54 percent—opposed the measure when it actually came before them. Some, motivated by religious arguments, feared it would undermine the sanctity of life. Others favored euthanasia but questioned whether this proposal had too many loopholes.

Among the issues that disturbed the opponents of the proposition were these: Can physicians really know patients' wishes? Can they accurately diagnose and predict how much time is left? Might not patients mistakenly labeled as terminal choose to die needlessly? Would the elderly choose suicide—or even be pushed into death—simply to spare their families' energies, emotions, and pocketbooks?

The Washington vote hardly ended Americans' anguish over the process of dying. A *Boston Globe* poll showed that 64 percent of the public favors letting doctors give lethal injections to the terminally ill; Derek Humphry's *Final Exit*, a handbook on how to commit suicide, achieved bestseller status. And other states have prepared new and improved versions of initiative 119; the first such measure was voted down by Californians in the 1992 elections.

A Great Debate

The fact is that the euthanasia issue, especially when linked to the controversy over abortion, has emerged as one of the great debates in turn-of-the-century America; the public must choose between the various "right to life" and "pro-choice" arguments as they apply to death as well as to birth. . . .

Should society remain aloof from the decision [to choose death], or should policy establish the ground rules governing the individual, his or her family, and the medical profession? . . .

Current opponents of death with dignity [sometimes called rational suicide] believe that society must maintain the taboo against suicide because the right to choose one's own death can quickly become mixed up with the right to "choose" someone else's. Were suicide to be legalized, these people foresee a quick descent into other forms of euthanasia, an unreasonable expansion of the powers of physicians, and an increase in state control over life. Indeed, during the debate over initiative 119, Washingtonians made clear their concern over these possibilities. Many Americans approve of death with dignity for themselves but fear taking the grave step of giving physicians or the state lethal power over others.

When we consider euthanasia as a public policy, we must directly confront these issues. In California and the other states to follow, the clash over current medical and legal arrangements for death will undoubtedly raise such stark problems as these:

- Should the "right" to die extend to those who have already lost the mental capacity to choose for themselves? Opponents of rational suicide believe that allowing such an option would open the door to eliminating everyone deemed

153

"unfit." To avoid reviving the nightmare of Nazism, proponents of euthanasia must clearly affirm the principle of autonomy: the conscious, free, and consenting person must make the original choice of terminating life. "Living wills" and the protections afforded by initiative 119 must guarantee that the patient voluntarily and intentionally requested assistance in death before an incapacitating illness or coma occurred. Such a provision would bar the door to experiments in eugenics and would, in fact, impose stricter restrictions on the "right to die" than now exist in many states.

- Should persons afflicted with serious conditions but who are not near death be allowed to end their lives? Proponents contend that people who are still able to choose but who are physically helpless (such as paraplegics) and those who are diagnosed as being on the brink of an inexorable decline (such as Alzheimer patients) should be allowed to consider suicide as a viable option. Opponents contend that such a concession would open the door for the mentally unstable, the temporarily depressed, or the immature to end their lives prematurely.

Protecting the Mentally Ill

Clearly, people who pass through a period of clinical depression often entertain the idea of suicide but reject it when they are properly treated. Similarly, a large number of American teenagers—roughly one in twelve high-school students (grades nine to twelve)—say that they have tried to commit suicide at least once. (In fact, the rate of actual suicide is much lower than for the elderly and those with degenerative diseases.) Nonetheless, the fact remains that temporarily dejected people—for example, teenagers who have separated from someone they love—or even revengeful persons do commit suicide. While it will be impossible to prevent all of these deaths, an argument for the right to die with dignity does not mean that society would make it easy for the deranged, irrational person to end life capriciously.

To guard against this, public policy should provide that only mature, mentally competent adults with acceptable reasons are allowed to make the decision—and then only after a certain waiting period. Before a person's request for assistance in dying is approved by a public body, it would be wise to have psychologists or psychiatrists consult with the patient and explore all of the options open to that person. While such an approach would screen out some disturbed, impetuous, harassed, or temporarily dejected patients, it would allow people who rationally anticipate a life of misery to choose death with dignity.

Some other issues to consider:

- Should physicians be in charge of the actual death? Their

oath requires them to prolong life; if they shorten it, this sends an ambiguous message to the society. Thus, in general, physicians should not be directly involved in ending life—certainly less so than they are now. In the termination of feeding or, indeed, in capital punishment, Kevorkian has suggested that doctors should not use his suicide machine; instead, consistent with the principles of autonomy and dignity, the patients themselves (or trusted relatives) must take the final action. Kevorkian envisions suicide clinics administered by paramedical workers who would be salaried so that there would be no profit motive involved.

- What if doctors make a mistake? Inevitably, doctors may miscalculate their diagnoses or a "miracle" may extend the life of a hopeless patient. Conceivably, a new treatment could result in unexpected cures (although the lag between the discovery of a beneficial therapy and its application is seldom less than a year). This is unquestionably one of the great risks of medical practice, and it suggests again that the role of the physician should be minimized; the doctor should be an expert counselor but not the person who controls or executes the decision. The burden of the choice must be borne by the patient; the exercise of an individual's autonomy should be that person's sole responsibility.

Sparing the Family

- If rational suicide were freely and broadly allowed, would the elderly, terminally ill, or even seriously ill choose it simply to spare their families' lives and pocketbooks? Possibly. Like the terminally ill in pre-modern Eskimo society, patients might well act out of consideration and compassion for their families. Such self-sacrifice should not be condemned as necessarily evil, but it must not be undertaken lightly. As in other cases, a frank, open, and loving consultation between patient and family should precede any action.

- Is there a grisly possibility that someone—even a person's own family—could push that person into suicide against his or her will? Is it possible that a murder could be hidden as suicide? This could occur—as indeed it already does. The Dutch experience [in which the widespread practice of euthanasia has not led to a devaluation of human life], however, indicates that the legitimation of rational suicide does not *increase* this possibility. With the safeguards proposed even in initiative 119, it seems reasonable to suppose that the chances of murder masked as suicide would actually be decreased.

- Doesn't the hospice movement offer a better alternative than rational suicide? It certainly provides an important alternative and a humane mode of coping with death under circumstances of relatively little pain. However, whether it is better to perish slowly, benumbed by morphine cocktails, or to be allowed to choose the mode, manner, and timing of one's death is, in the opinion of this author, a matter best left to individual discretion.

The obstacles to a public policy of euthanasia are admittedly formidable, but they are not insurmountable. A failure to decide these issues because of personal or social anguish over "contemplating the unthinkable" will continue to condemn many people to humiliating debility, pointless suffering, and perhaps meaningless "final exits." In contrast, sensible provisions for rational suicide—governed by the principles of autonomy, dignity, and compassion—offer humankind the possibility of ending a life that was so acceptable that it required no further deeds or days.

"Social scientists have an opportunity to . . . shed light on . . . circumstances under which assisted suicide might be morally justifiable."

Social Science Can Guide Decisions

William J. Winslade and Kyriakos S. Markides

William J. Winslade is James Wade Rockwell Professor of Philosophy of Medicine, professor of preventive medicine and community health, and professor of psychiatry and behavioral sciences at the University of Texas Medical Branch at Galveston. He is the author of *Choosing Life and Death*. Kyriakos S. Markides is a professor of preventive medicine and community health and director of the division of sociomedical sciences at the University of Texas Medical Branch at Galveston. He is the founding editor of the *Journal of Aging and Health*. In the following viewpoint, Winslade and Markides suggest that social scientists can contribute greatly to decisions concerning euthanasia.

As you read, consider the following questions:

1. Which of Jack Kevorkian's ideas and actions do the authors criticize? Which do they support?
2. What specific issues could social scientists research that would shed light on decisions concerning euthanasia, according to Winslade and Markides?
3. The success of medicine has always been measured by its ability to extend human life. What should be medicine's new goal, in the authors' opinion?

Reprinted by permission of Transaction Publishers from William J. Winslade and Kyriakos S. Markides, "Assisted Suicide and Professional Responsibilities," *Society*, July/August 1992. Copyright ©1992 by Transaction Publishers.

A seventy-nine-year-old woman with late stage Parkinson's disease is mentally alert but physically crippled; she cannot feed herself, walk, or control her bowels and bladder. She deplores her disabilities and the poor quality of her life. Despite the affection and concern of her eighty-one-year-old husband, three children and several grandchildren, after more than two years in a nursing home she wants to die. Because she is physically unable to take her own life, she seeks help. Although she is unhappy about her disease and her condition, she is not clinically depressed. She is lucid, rational, and determined to die in her own way. Should her family or her physician give her aid in dying?

Immediately a cluster of questions arises: Is it illegal to facilitate a suicide? What are the ethical, religious, and professional issues for the family and physician? How would a participant feel about providing the means to commit suicide? How will the family feel about her death if it is a suicide? Will the nursing home be harmed if the suicide occurs while she is a resident there? If she does commit suicide must it be reported to the authorities for an official investigation? How desirable or likely is it that anyone who assists in suicide will be prosecuted for a crime? Does she really want to die or is she ambivalent? Would she change her mind if some aspect of her suffering could be modified? If she is fully competent, should her autonomy be respected? These are only some of the questions that must be answered. Even if the answer is yes in each instance, someone must actually provide the means. Even if the suicide occurs, someone must face the consequences of reporting the death. All those involved must deal with the immediate and lasting emotional impact of the death. Whenever assisted suicide occurs, complex interpersonal relationships and profound questions of ethics, law, and the meaning of human life create troubling issues for many professionals.

Everyone's Worries

It is difficult to know where to begin a discussion of terminal illness, the use of artificial life support, assisted suicide, and euthanasia. For more than fifteen years, Americans have been deluged with court cases, media attention, legislation, popular literature, and how-to-do-it books such as Derek Humphry's *Final Exit*. Our capacity to think clearly about these issues is threatened by a cacophony of voices that pose troubling but often ambiguous or poorly formulated questions. Misinformation, oversimplification, blind advocacy, institutional inertia, and emotional ambivalence about dying and death further thwart efforts to make sense of the issues. Academic analyses seem interminable and public policy debates remain inconclusive. Value conflicts about the "right to die" and the "right to life" polarize public discussions and paralyze legal debates.

It is not surprising that many of us are impatient with endless talk when decisions must be made and action must be taken. Patients, family members, and health professionals are confused about what actions are permitted or required, legal or illegal, ethical or unethical. Patients and their families are concerned about losing control of their lives not only to illness or injury, but to hospitals and bureaucracies with high costs and unfamiliar legal rules. Health professionals worry about government regulations, insurance issues, and malpractice suits. When patients do not improve or do get worse, decisions must be made about how aggressively the illness should be treated.

In hospitals and nursing homes decisions about the use of artificial life support system—ventilators, nutrition and hydration, and other procedures that will prolong life—are made daily. Less frequent, but symbolically significant, are decisions to assist suicide or perform euthanasia. Public opinion polls show that many people desire to have the option of assisted suicide or euthanasia. Distinguished physicians in the United States and Great Britain believe that it is permissible to provide aid in dying as a last resort. But attempts to legalize assisted suicide or euthanasia have failed in California and Oregon. The American Medical Association and the American Bar Association are strongly opposed.

The Mission of Jack Kevorkian

Despite continuing legal and moral controversy, some advocates of assisted suicide openly engage in it. In America, a physician, Jack Kevorkian, advocates assisted suicide and brings to the debate a loose collection of ideas about human experimentation, methods of capital punishment, and organ donation. He recently brought them together in his book *Prescription Medicide: The Goodness of Planned Death*. Kevorkian is someone who also puts his beliefs into action and is willing to face the consequences. He has openly assisted several people who have committed suicide. In 1990 he helped Janet Adkins, who was suffering from Alzheimer's disease, take her own life with the aid of his notorious "suicide machine." In 1991 two more women committed suicide with his assistance; one suffered from multiple sclerosis, the other from a painful pelvic disease. Kevorkian was charged with murder in the death of Janet Adkins, but the charges were dismissed because the state law in Michigan does not criminalize assisted suicide. . . .

Kevorkian believes that planned death, whether in the form of capital punishment or suicide in the face of illness, provides scientists with the opportunity to benefit from the dying process. Dying can be controlled and prolonged by anesthesia. After the person is rendered permanently unconscious, various procedures can be performed on the living human body, organs can be removed for transplantation, mysteries of dying can be explored, after which death can be brought about with a lethal dose of barbiturates. Such ideas are not merely eccentric, they are extremely radical and controversial. Although arguments in favor of such views may exist, Kevorkian is impatient with systematic rational discussion. He thinks it outrageous and wasteful that such unique opportunities for scientific research are not already being explored. He promotes his ideas and practices with total disregard of and contempt for institutional arrangements. Although he is right that regulations impede scientific progress, he ignores the fact that regulations also protect the vulnerable from exploitation and prevent researchers from overreaching themselves.

The Case of Janet Adkins

With regard to assisted suicide and euthanasia for seriously ill patients, Kevorkian mentions the case of a middle-aged woman dying of cancer whose body was ravaged by the disease. Unfortunately, he does not tell enough about the case for us to know whether the patient did, might, or would have sought assisted suicide or euthanasia. He only tells about his empathy for her suffering. When discussing cases other than that of Janet Adkins, Kevorkian offers only cryptic and often superficial commentary. This is particularly troubling because the strongest argument for assisted suicide can be made when particular cases are described in sufficient detail to bring out their rational and moral justification. In the case of Janet Adkins, Kevorkian does present evidence that she was acting on her own initiative, was competent, and truly wanted his assistance in ending her life. She wanted to control the time, place, and manner of her death. He apparently responded to her need and ardent desire in a humane, sensitive, and caring way. Moreover, he was willing to face the legal, professional, and social consequences of his action. He certainly was subjected to considerable criticism, the stress of criminal litigation, and to professional scrutiny. But he also garnered considerable support and praise for acting publicly on the basis of his personal and professional beliefs and in response to a sincere request.

If Kevorkian argued only that certain cases of assisted suicide can be morally justified and should be carried out where legally permissible, one might have little disagreement. But he advocates much more. He believes that if assisted suicide became a "legitimate medical service everywhere, medicine would soon reduce substantially the increasing rate of suicide for all age groups, especially the elderly." There may be some merit to

Kevorkian's claim that having the option of assisted suicide may influence suicide rates, but he offers no reliable evidence for his position. Similarly his views about why people commit suicide are unsupported speculation. His book draws very selectively on a small body of literature to give it the appearance of scholarship, but in fact the book is a passionate plea for conclusions that he accepts as axioms rather than as positions arrived at through rational argument and evidence.

Cause for Alarm

Kevorkian endorses the idea of a cadre of medically, or at least technically, trained persons who could assist suicides. He envisions "suicide centers" where "medicide" (euthanasia or assisted suicide performed by professionals) could be provided. And a new medical specialty, "obitiatry," for the study of dying, experimentation, salvaging of organs could be practiced. His proposal far exceeds Robin Cook's morbid entrepreneurial imagination in *Coma*, a medical mystery novel in which patients are rendered permanently unconscious so their bodies can be harvested for tissues and organs. Kevorkian appears less interested in assisted suicide and more fascinated with unravelling the mystery of life and death by dissecting unconscious, yet living bodies. Kevorkian's book does a disservice to those of his ideas that have some plausibility because it reads more like a *Bizarro* or a *Far Side* cartoon than a serious, scientific treatise.

Kevorkian's actions, like those of the Dutch physician Pieter Admiraal, are cause for alarm. Both physicians are noted more for their advocacy and their passion than for their reasoning. Both ardently support the notion of an institutionalized, assisted suicide service. Admiraal operates out of a hospital in Delft while Kevorkian has used his Volkswagen van and an isolated cabin in a state park. In America, one can imagine that such services might even be franchised; some have even morbidly joked that a drive-thru McDeath could be offered to those who are in a hurry.

Inspired by his visit with Admiraal in Holland, Kevorkian's plan was at first to offer assisted suicide to terminally ill patients. He explains that he chose assisted suicide rather than euthanasia because the former is not a crime in Michigan. However, he is apparently not limiting assisted suicide to terminally ill patients, for as the case of Janet Adkins illustrates, chronic degenerative illness seems enough. He would also assist the suicide of condemned prisoners, certain incapacitated patients, including those incapable of informed consent, and others who merely seek "rational" suicide. One obvious problem with Kevorkian's expanded view of a "suicide center" is that it lends itself to enormous potential for bad judgment, exploitation, or evil. He offers no serious suggestion about how one might properly regulate or restrain the activities at such centers. In fact, he thinks that any type of regulation should be handled only by medical professionals, not by legislators, courts, or other public officials.

Kevorkian's Insensitivity

Kevorkian's provocative words are completely unsupported by evidence or argument. One also wonders whether his actions in particular situations are as arbitrary as his intellectual pronouncements. Although his handling of the Janet Adkins case seemed to show circumspection and justification, one wonders whether his subsequent assisted suicides were as carefully thought through. One of the dangers of routinizing such a personally and symbolically significant event is that one may become callous and careless in attending to the moral, psychological, and social nuances of medicide. This is especially problematic if one has an ideological agenda and a social reform mission. Respect for the individual patient's needs, desires, and autonomy may give way to the utilitarian goal that Kevorkian explicitly affirms, "to extract benefit from death." The individual may be sacrificed for the good of the science of "obitiatry."

Advocates of assisted suicide discourage rational and responsible debate about topics that warrant careful and detailed discussion. Kevorkian's dogmatic outbursts, similar to those of Derek Humphry, promote ideological controversy at the expense of clear thinking or responsible conduct. By disregarding complex facts, values, and feelings in particular cases and in public policy formulations, he, like Humphry, undermines the credibility of his proposals. Those of us who are inclined to support a more tolerant attitude toward assisted suicide or euthanasia and are even sympathetic to limited legal permissibility are frustrated by such intemperateness and superficiality. Legal reform and modification of medical practice are not matters for rhetorical excess; they merit serious and thoughtful reflection.

Kevorkian's book is a shallow and fanatic diatribe mixed with occasional insights and moments of humanitarian concern. It is unfortunate that he espouses ideas that make him appear not only eccentric but outright dangerous. It is, therefore, not surprising that he should have been prosecuted again, even if he did not commit murder or violate a specific law against assisted suicide. We have given Kevorkian so much attention because he is a dominant figure in the public debate on assisted suicide. Publicity surrounding his views and actions has at last launched a serious debate among scholars that may also reach a popular audience. Scholarly discussions on assisted suicide have been held primarily among ethicists, lawyers, and health professionals with social scientists only now beginning to pay adequate attention to the issues involved. Social scientists can contribute to the debate in a number of ways, but mostly through research on assisted suicide.

Issues to Consider

Researchable issues include: 1) Are those who request assistance to commit suicide tired of living or are they terminally ill? 2) What is the relationship of mental illness to requests for assisted suicide? 3) What is the impact of assisted suicide on family members? 4) How do the views of family members toward (assisted) suicide change after the event takes place? 5) How does the quality of life of dying patients influence their attitudes toward assisted suicide? 6) What are the attitudes of medical professionals toward assisted suicide and euthanasia? 7) How well does the public understand the issues involved? This research must go beyond simple opinion polls to gain in-depth information on the public's views and attitudes.

Choosing suicide, whether assisted or not, is a complex and very personal decision. Despite Emile Durkheim's classic work *Suicide*, one of the first serious social epidemiologic studies, our understanding of why and under what conditions people will commit suicide remains superficial. A major problem preventing better knowledge is the impracticality of following up large cohorts of people to see who will commit suicide. In the case of assisted suicide, where a decision to terminate one's life has been made, the job of the researcher is easier because the population is well defined. Given the aging of our society and the increase of terminally ill patients, suicide, both assisted and unassisted, is likely to increase. Social scientists have an opportunity to study this phenomenon, not to help prevent suicide at all cost, but to shed light on conditions and circumstances under which assisted suicide might be morally justifiable and personally and socially preferable.

The successes of modern medicine and science have been measured by their ability to extend life. With life expectancy moving ever closer to its biological limits, a more appropriate concern would be to what extent we can enhance or maintain the quality of life of the rising number of disabled elderly people. At what point the quality is so greatly diminished that life to them is no longer worth living is an extremely personal and complex question that will increasingly challenge our social institutions. Understanding this challenge and communicating the issues to the public is an important responsibility of social scientists as it is of legal experts, ethicists, and health professionals.

====
"Euthanasia . . . is self-determination run amok."
====

No One Has the Right to Make Decisions in Support of Euthanasia

Daniel Callahan

No one has the right to choose euthanasia, and society does not have the right to permit deaths by euthanasia, Daniel Callahan argues in the following viewpoint. Euthanasia is simply a form of killing, Callahan believes. He opposes all killing and maintains that, should euthanasia be legalized, patients, families, and physicians would abuse this power to kill. Callahan, a medical ethicist and writer, is the director of the Hastings Center, a Briarcliff Manor, New York, think tank that focuses on biomedical ethics and health care.

As you read, consider the following questions:

1. Why does Callahan oppose the concept of self-determination as a reason for euthanasia?
2. How do the concepts of causality and culpability relate to euthanasia, in the author's opinion?
3. How would involving physicians in euthanasia affect medicine, in Callahan's opinion?

From Daniel Callahan, "When Self-Determination Runs Amok," *Hastings Center Report*, March/April 1992. Reprinted by permission; © The Hastings Center.

The euthanasia debate is not just another moral debate, one in a long list of arguments in our pluralistic society. It is profoundly emblematic of three important turning points in Western thought. The first is that of the legitimate conditions under which one person can kill another. The acceptance of voluntary active euthanasia would morally sanction what can only be called "consenting adult killing." By that term I mean the killing of one person by another in the name of their mutual right to be killer and killed if they freely agree to play those roles. This turn flies in the face of a longstanding effort to limit the circumstances under which one person can take the life of another, from efforts to control the free flow of guns and arms, efforts to abolish capital punishment and to more tightly control warfare. Euthanasia would add a whole new category of killing to a society that already has too many excuses to indulge itself in that way.

The second turning point lies in the meaning and limits of self-determination. The acceptance of euthanasia would sanction a view of autonomy holding that individuals may, in the name of their own private, idiosyncratic view of the good life, call upon others, including such institutions as medicine, to help them pursue that life, even at the risk of harm to the common good. This works against the idea that the meaning and scope of our own right to lead our own lives must be conditioned by, and be compatible with, the good of the community, which is more than an aggregate of self-directing individuals.

The third point is to be found in the claim being made upon medicine: it should be prepared to make its skills available to individuals to help them achieve their private vision of the good life. This puts medicine in the business of promoting the individualistic pursuit of general human happiness and well-being. It would overturn the traditional belief that medicine should limit its domain to promoting and preserving human health, redirecting it instead to the relief of that suffering which stems from life itself, not merely from a sick body.

I believe that, at each of these three turning points, proponents of euthanasia push us in the wrong direction. Arguments in favor of euthanasia fall into four general categories, which I will take up in turn: (1) the moral claim of individual self-determination and well-being; (2) the moral irrelevance of the difference between killing and allowing to die; (3) the supposed paucity of evidence to show likely harmful consequences of legalized euthanasia; and (4) the compatibility of euthanasia and medical practice.

Self-Determination

Central to most arguments for euthanasia is the principle of self-determination. People are presumed to have an interest in deciding for themselves, according to their own beliefs about what makes life good, how they will conduct their lives. That is an important value, but the question in the euthanasia context is, What does it mean and how far should it extend? If it were a question of suicide, where a person takes her own life without assistance from another, that principle might be pertinent, at least for debate. But euthanasia is not that limited a matter. The self-determination in that case can only be effected by the moral and physical assistance of another. Euthanasia is thus no longer a matter only of self-determination, but of a mutual, social decision between two people, the one to be killed and the other to do the killing.

How are we to make the moral move from my right of self-determination to some doctor's right to kill me—from *my* right to *his* right? Where does the doctor's moral warrant to kill come from? Ought doctors to be able to kill anyone they want as long as permission is given by competent persons? Is our right to life just like a piece of property, to be given away or alienated if the price (happiness, relief of suffering) is right? And then to be destroyed with our permission once alienated?

Pontius' Puddle

Reprinted by permission of Joel Kauffmann.

In answer to all those questions, I will say this: I have yet to hear a plausible argument why it should be permissible for us to put this kind of power in the hands of another, whether a doctor or anyone else. The idea that we can waive our right to life, and then give to another the power to take that life, requires a justification yet to be provided by anyone.

Slavery was long ago outlawed on the ground that one person should not have the right to own another, even with the other's permission. Why? Because it is a fundamental moral wrong for one person to give over his life and fate to another, whatever the good consequences, and no less a wrong for another person to have that kind of total, final power. Like slavery, dueling was long ago banned on similar grounds: even free, competent individuals should not have the power to kill each other, whatever their motives, whatever the circumstances. Consenting adult killing, like consenting adult slavery or degradation, is a strange route to human dignity.

There is another problem as well. If doctors, once sanctioned to carry out euthanasia, are to be themselves responsible moral agents—not simply hired hands with lethal injections at the ready—then they must have their own *independent* moral grounds to kill those who request such services. What do I mean? As those who favor euthanasia are quick to point out, some people want it because their life has become so burdensome it no longer seems worth living.

The doctor will have a difficulty at this point. The degree and intensity to which people suffer from their diseases and their dying, and whether they find life more of a burden than a benefit, has very little directly to do with the nature or extent of their actual physical condition. Three people can have the same condition, but only one will find the suffering unbearable. People suffer, but suffering is as much a function of the values of individuals as it is of the physical causes of that suffering. Inevitably in that circumstance, the doctor will in effect be treating the patient's values. To be responsible, the doctor would have to share those values. The doctor would have to decide, on her own, whether the patient's life was "no longer worth living."

But how could a doctor possibly know that or make such a judgment? Just because the patient said so? I raise this question because, while in Holland at the euthanasia conference reported by Maurice de Wachter, the doctors present agreed that there is no objective way of measuring or judging the claims of patients that their suffering is unbearable. And if it is difficult to measure suffering, how much more difficult to determine the value of a patient's statement that her life is not worth living?

However one might want to answer such questions, the very need to ask them, to inquire into the physician's responsibility and grounds for medical and moral judgment, points out the social nature of the decision. Euthanasia is not a private matter of self-determination. It is an act that requires two people to make it possible, and a complicit society to make it acceptable.

Killing and Allowing to Die

Against common opinion, the argument is sometimes made that there is no moral difference between stopping life-sustaining treatment and more active forms of killing, such as lethal injection. Instead I would contend that the notion that there is no morally significant difference between omission and commission is just wrong. Consider in its broad implications what the eradication of the distinction implies: that death from disease has been banished, leaving only the actions of physicians in terminating treatment as the cause of death. Biology, which used to bring about death, has apparently been displaced by human agency. Doctors have finally, I suppose, thus genuinely become gods, now doing what nature and the deities once did.

What is the mistake here? It lies in confusing causality and culpability, and in failing to note the way in which human societies have overlaid natural causes with moral rules and interpretations. Causality (by which I mean the direct physical causes of death) and culpability (by which I mean our attribution of moral responsibility to human actions) are confused under three circumstances.

A Serious Mistake

It would be a grave (no pun intended) mistake for us to surrender to society in collusion with medical agents the right to decide whether those unable to speak or communicate should be shuffled out of their beds and into their graves. Just how much real determination of the cerebral state of such patients would enter into such decisions? And even then, would it be as infallible as a society eager to be unburdened by the imperfect might wish?

Karen Ann Quinlan lived nearly 10 years after physicians said she would die if taken off a respirator, such being allowed by court decision. True, she never returned to full consciousness as far as I know. But there have been other cases where patients did—suddenly and inexplicably—wake up even after years of only subconscious or unconscious existence.

Frank Morriss, *The Wanderer*, August 4, 1994.

They are confused, first, when the action of a physician in stopping treatment of a patient with an underlying lethal disease is construed as *causing* death. On the contrary, the physician's omission can only bring about death on the condition that the patient's disease will kill him in the absence of treatment. We may hold the physician morally responsible for the death, if we have morally judged such actions wrongful omissions. But it confuses reality and moral judgment to see an omitted action as having the same causal status as one that directly kills. A lethal injection will kill both a healthy person and a sick person. A physician's omitted treatment will have no effect on a healthy person. Turn off the machine on me, a healthy person, and nothing will happen. It will only, in contrast, bring the life of a sick person to an end because of an underlying fatal disease.

Causality and culpability are confused, second, when we fail to note that judgments of moral responsibility and culpability are human constructs. By that I mean that we human beings, after moral reflection, have decided to call some actions right or wrong, and to devise moral rules to deal with them. When physicians could do nothing to stop death, they were not held responsible for it. When, with medical progress, they began to have some power over death—but only its timing and circumstances, not its ultimate inevitability—moral rules were devised to set forth their obligations. Natural causes of death were not thereby banished. They were, instead, overlaid with a medical ethics designed to determine moral culpability in deploying medical power.

To confuse the judgments of this ethics with the physical causes of death—which is the connotation of the word *kill*—is to confuse nature and human action. People will, one way or another, die of some disease; death will have dominion over all of us. To say that a doctor "kills" a patient by allowing this to happen should only be understood as a moral judgment about the licitness of his omission, nothing more. We can, as a fashion of speech only, talk about a doctor *killing* a patient by omitting treatment he should have provided. It is a fashion of speech precisely because it is the underlying disease that brings death when treatment is omitted; that is its cause, not the physician's omission. It is a misuse of the word *killing* to use it when a doctor stops a treatment he believes will no longer benefit the patient—when, that is, he steps aside to allow an eventually inevitable death to occur now rather than later. The only deaths that human beings invented are those that come from direct killing—when, with a lethal injection, we both cause death and are morally responsible for it. In the case of omissions, we do not cause death even if we may be judged morally responsible for it.

Killing and Not Killing

The difference between causality and culpability also helps us see why a doctor who has omitted a treatment he should have provided has "killed" that patient while another doctor—performing precisely the same act of omission on another patient in different circumstances—does not kill her, but only allows her to die. The difference is that we have come, by moral convention and conviction, to classify unauthorized or illegitimate omissions as acts of "killing." We call them "killing" in the expanded sense of the term: a culpable action that permits the real cause of death, the underlying disease, to proceed to its lethal conclusion. By contrast, the doctor who, at the patient's request, omits or terminates unwanted treatment does not kill at all. Her underlying disease, not his action, is the physical cause of death; and we have agreed to consider actions of that kind to be morally licit. He thus can truly be said to have "allowed" her to die.

If we fail to maintain the distinction between killing and allowing to die, moreover, there are some disturbing possibilities. The first would be to confirm many physicians in their already too-powerful belief that, when patients die or when physicians stop treatment because of the futility of continuing it, they are somehow both morally and physically responsible for the deaths that follow. That notion needs to be abolished, not strengthened. It needlessly and wrongly burdens the physician, to whom should not be attributed the powers of the gods. The second possibility would be that, in every case where a doctor judges medical treatment no longer effective in prolonging life, a quick and direct killing of the patient would be seen as the next, most reasonable step, on grounds of both humaneness and economics. I do not see how that logic could easily be rejected.

Calculating the Consequences

When concerns about the adverse social consequences of permitting euthanasia are raised, its advocates tend to dismiss them as unfounded and overly speculative. On the contrary, recent data about the Dutch experience suggests that such concerns are right on target. From my own discussions in Holland, and from the articles on that subject, I believe we can now fully see most of the *likely* consequences of legal euthanasia.

Three consequences seem almost certain, in this or any other country: the inevitability of some abuse of the law; the difficulty of precisely writing, and then enforcing, the law; and the inherent slipperiness of the moral reasons for legalizing euthanasia in the first place.

Why is abuse inevitable? One reason is that almost all laws on delicate, controversial matters are to some extent abused. This happens because not everyone will agree with the law as written and will bend it, or ignore it, if they can get away with it. From explicit admissions to me by Dutch proponents of euthanasia, and from the corroborating information provided by the Remmelink Report and the outside studies of Carlos Gomez and John Keown, I am convinced that in the Netherlands there are a substantial number of cases of nonvoluntary euthanasia, that is, euthanasia undertaken without the explicit permission of the person being killed. The other reason abuse is inevitable is that the law is likely to have a low enforcement priority in the criminal justice system. Like other laws of similar status, unless there is an unrelenting and harsh willingness to pursue abuse, violations will ordinarily be tolerated. The worst thing to me about my experience

170

in Holland was the casual, seemingly indifferent attitude toward abuse. I think that would happen everywhere.

Meaningful Law Is Impossible to Enforce

Why would it be hard to precisely write, and then enforce, the law? The Dutch speak about the requirement of "unbearable" suffering, but admit that such a term is just about indefinable, a highly subjective matter admitting of no objective standards. A requirement for outside opinion is nice, but it is easy to find complaisant colleagues. A requirement that a medical condition be "terminal" will run aground on the notorious difficulties of knowing when an illness is actually terminal.

Apart from those technical problems there is a more profound worry. I see no way, even in principle, to write or enforce a meaningful law that can guarantee effective procedural safeguards. The reason is obvious yet almost always overlooked. The euthanasia transaction will ordinarily take place within the boundaries of the private and confidential doctor-patient relationship. No one can possibly know what takes place in that context unless the doctor chooses to reveal it. In Holland, less than 10 percent of the physicians report their acts of euthanasia and do so with almost complete legal impunity. There is no reason why the situation should be any better elsewhere. Doctors will have their own reasons for keeping euthanasia secret, and some patients will have no less a motive for wanting it concealed.

I would mention, finally, that the moral logic of the motives for euthanasia contain within them the ingredients of abuse. The two standard motives for euthanasia and assisted suicide are said to be our right of self-determination, and our claim upon the mercy of others, especially doctors, to relieve our suffering. These two motives are typically spliced together and presented as a single justification. Yet if they are considered independently—and there is no inherent reason why they must be linked—they reveal serious problems. It is said that a competent, adult person should have a right to euthanasia for the relief of suffering. But why must the person be suffering? Does not that stipulation already compromise the principle of self-determination? How can self-determination have any limits? Whatever the person's motives may be, why are they not sufficient?

Consider next the person who is suffering but not competent, who is perhaps demented or mentally retarded. The standard argument would deny euthanasia to that person. But why? If a person is suffering but not competent, then it would seem grossly unfair to deny relief solely on the grounds of incompetence. Are the incompetent less entitled to relief from suffering than the competent? Will it only be affluent, middle-class people, mentally fit and savvy about working the medical system, who can qualify? Do the incompetent suffer less because of their incompetence?

Considered from these angles, there are no good moral reasons to limit euthanasia once the principle of taking life for that purpose has been legitimated. If we really believe in self-determination, then any competent person should have a right to be killed by a doctor for any reason that suits him. If we believe in the relief of suffering, then it seems cruel and capricious to deny it to the incompetent. There is, in short, no reasonable or logical stopping point once the turn has been made down the road to euthanasia, which could soon turn into a convenient and commodious expressway. . . .

Euthanasia and Medical Practice

The root problem of illness and mortality is both medical and philosophical or religious. "Why must I die?" can be asked as a technical, biological question or as a question about the meaning of life. When medicine tries to respond to the latter, which it is always under pressure to do, it moves beyond its proper role.

It is not medicine's place to lift from us the burden of that suffering which turns on the meaning we assign to the decay of the body and its eventual death. It is not medicine's place to determine when lives are not worth living or when the burden of life is too great to be borne. Doctors have no conceivable way of evaluating such claims on the part of patients, and they should have no right to act in response to them. Medicine should try to relieve human suffering, but only that suffering which is brought on by illness and dying as biological phenomena, not that suffering which comes from anguish or despair at the human condition.

Doctors ought to relieve those forms of suffering that medically accompany serious illness and the threat of death. They should relieve pain, do what they can to allay anxiety and uncertainty, and be a comforting presence. As sensitive human beings, doctors should be prepared to respond to patients who ask why they must die, or die in pain. But here the doctor and the patient are at the same level. The doctor may have no better answer to those old questions than anyone else; and certainly no special insight from his training as a physician. It would be terrible for physicians to forget this, and to think that in a swift, lethal injection, medicine has found its own answer to the riddle of life. . . . The problem is precisely that, too often in human history, killing has seemed the quick, efficient way to put aside that which burdens us. It rarely helps, and too often simply adds to one evil still another. That is what I believe euthanasia would accomplish. It is self-determination run amok.

Periodical Bibliography

The following articles have been selected to supplement the diverse views presented in this chapter.

John J. Conley — "Masks of Autonomy," *Society*, July/August 1992.

Ezekiel J. Emanuel — "A Communal Vision of Care of Incompetent Patients," *Hastings Center Report*, November 1987.

Mike Ervin — "Who Gets to Live? Who Will Decide?" *The Progressive*, October 1994.

Bernard Gert, James L. Bernat, and R. Peter Mogielnicki — "Distinguishing Between Patients' Refusals and Requests," *Hastings Center Report*, July/August 1994.

Kathryn A. Koch et al. — "Analysis of Power in Medical Decision-Making: An Argument for Physician Autonomy," *Law, Medicine & Health Care*, Winter 1992. Available from 765 Commonwealth Ave., Suite 1634, Boston, MA 02215.

Ed Larson and Beth Spring — "Life-Defying Acts," *Christianity Today*, March 6, 1987.

Gerald A. Larue — "Euthanasia: The Time Is Now," *Free Inquiry*, Winter 1988-89. Available from PO Box 5, Buffalo, NY 14215.

Jonathan D. Moreno — "Who's to Choose?" *Hastings Center Report*, January/February 1993.

Frank Morriss — "Let Them Die," *The Wanderer*, August 4, 1994. Available from 201 Ohio St., St. Paul, MN 55107.

Edmund D. Pellegrino — "Life and Death Decisions: Do You Trust Yourself to Play God?" *U.S. Catholic*, October 1987.

Julian Savulescu — "Treatment Limitation Decisions Under Uncertainty: The Value of Subsequent Euthanasia," *Bioethics*, January 1994. Available from Basil Blackwell, 238 Main St., Suite 501, Cambridge, MA 02142.

Mildred Z. Solomon — "How Physicians Talk About Futility: Making Words Mean Too Many Things," *Journal of Law, Medicine & Ethics*, Summer 1993. Available from 765 Commonwealth Ave., Suite 1634, Boston, MA 02215.

Ellen Sweet — "Deciding How to Die," *Ms.*, July 1986.

Is Infant
Euthanasia Ethical?

Euthanasia

Chapter Preface

In July 1993 Siamese twins Angela and Amy Lakeberg were born. The twins, fused at the chest, shared a heart and a liver. They were given no chance of survival without surgery; with surgery, one would have a very small chance. Physicians in Philadelphia decided to separate the twins and give the organs to Angela, allowing Amy to die during surgery. Eleven months later Angela died, having spent her entire life in the hospital attached to a respirator.

Critics questioned whether treating the twins was ethical or practical. Was the small chance of saving one twin worth the extreme expense of the surgery and Angela's subsequent care? Was it ethical to allow one twin to live at the expense of the other? And, finally, was it ethical to put the twins and their parents through the physical and emotional trauma of the decision and the surgery?

The Lakeberg case was very unusual. But some of the issues it raised are faced daily by the parents and physicians of severely ill newborns—those with anencephaly, severe spina bifida, and other disorders. Handicapped infants are perhaps the most vulnerable members of society. Family law attorney Julie Koenig calls severely ill newborns "the weakest class of human beings." As such, she and others believe these infants deserve as much protection as possible—including protection from euthanasia. Koenig argues that allowing parents and physicians to perform euthanasia on infants would "irrevocably damage the fabric of our lives, the protections of our laws and the character of our civilization." Physicians and parents who share Koenig's views do everything in their power to save the life of a newborn, even if the chance for long-term survival and health is slim.

But other parents, physicians, and health care experts argue that protecting a newborn's interests may in some cases mean allowing or helping the child to die. This may be the most ethical choice, some insist, if the child faces little or no hope of survival and if the child would have to endure the pain and discomfort of treatment for little or no benefit. John Freeman, an expert on spina bifida, believes that "active euthanasia might be the most humane course for the *most severely* affected infants."

What is best for the severely handicapped newborn is often difficult to determine. In the following chapter, the contributors debate whether euthanasia is ever an ethical option for such an infant.

"Change the law so that families of anencephalic babies receive comfort from the knowledge that an opportunity exists to give life to others."

Euthanizing Anencephalic Infants for Their Organs Is Ethical

Robert J. Lerer

Infants born with anencephaly have little or no brain, but usually have other organs that are healthy. Such infants usually live a few days. If the infants are euthanized while their organs are still healthy, these organs can be donated to other children. In the following viewpoint, Robert J. Lerer supports this practice. Euthanizing anencephalic babies is a way of gaining some benefit from a tragic situation, he believes. It would comfort the grieving parents and perhaps save the lives of many ill children. Lerer is a pediatrician in a group private practice in Fairfield, Ohio.

As you read, consider the following questions:

1. What happened to the first anencephalic infant the author treated?
2. What prevents physicians from simply waiting for anencephalic babies to die before harvesting their organs, according to Lerer?
3. Why did Lerer's hospital refuse to allow the Amalfis to donate their child's organs?

Robert J. Lerer, "Praying for Legal Wisdom to Allow New Life from Tragedy," *American Medical News*, November 2, 1992. Reprinted by permission of the author.

I could tell right away that the baby's cranium was caved in. In spite of a generous amount of thick black hair, my tiny newborn patient, not yet a minute old, was born with little underlying brain tissue. Her facial features looked adorable. All her other organ systems had formed normally and would function for a few days or weeks. But then this newest patient of mine would die.

And this she did a couple of weeks later. But not before creating quite a stir in my hospital, practice and community.

Prenatal Diagnosis

I have attended the births of perhaps a dozen babies with anencephaly over the 22 years since I finished medical school. In the "old days" such disorders often presented themselves at birth, but now, with the advent of alpha-fetoprotein screening antenatally and ultrasound monitoring during pregnancy, I often know the diagnosis before delivery. Since the brain stem is spared in this congenital anomaly, the baby can maintain vital functions until death occurs from infection, malnutrition or respiratory arrest. With no hope for reasonable survival, these babies are allowed to die.

As I was attending this newest patient, my thoughts flashed back to my first one. She had created a stir also: She was purposefully suffocated by an overzealous house officer, who meant to avoid pain for the baby and her family. It cost the resident her job—mercy killing would not be tolerated. My next case occurred a few weeks after the first, and the poor baby took three weeks to die a horrible, painful death with incurable meningitis. Because of the previous case, we dared not withhold any support measures. I hated to see the suffering of the baby and his family day after day.

Baby Girl Amalfi—I'm not using real names—was the first baby for a storybook couple, both professionals and active in community and church. The mother was a wonderful patient, who learned early from her obstetrician that the baby she carried had anencephaly. She refused an abortion on religious grounds and continued all preventive visits and advice. Thus, the staff caring for mother and baby were prepared for the birth and the expected psychological, ethical, legal and medical considerations.

Parents Wished to Donate Organs

The delivery was uneventful, and after an assessment I handed the newborn back to her mother and father (who had attended her birth as well) so they could bond with her. I gently wrapped the shriveled-up head with a warm receiving blanket, and she already looked like an angel.

The Amalfis wished to donate the baby's organs for transplantation soon after the delivery, so the tissues would not have a chance to deteriorate. They had done their research and realized that the gradual decline in function and the infections make organs unsuitable for safe transplantation. I knew that the longer we waited, the less likely our chances would be to succeed in complying with their wishes.

The hospital chaplain had been alerted to this family's needs. He believed that if the baby were declared brain dead in the legal sense, then the necessary surgery could take place, and the baby would then expire, presumably in painless and humane fashion. He saw no violation of religious ethics and shared a belief with the family that this might be the only way to extend life for the child. "Our baby will be able to live through others," the father told me. Also, it would be more humane, the couple thought, for her to die during surgery than slowly and painfully following life support.

The Facts About Anencephaly

What is it? A neural tube defect in which the failure of the neural groove to close normally early in pregnancy leads to lack of brain development, and all or a major part of the brain is absent.

How common is it? Very rare in full-term babies, since 99 percent of fetuses with the defect are miscarried.

Who is susceptible? Not known.

What causes it? Not known at present. Heredity is probably involved in some way, along with adverse prenatal environment.

Related problems. All body systems are affected negatively.

Treatment. None, and most doctors agree that no medical intervention is best, though the baby should be kept as comfortable as possible.

Prognosis. The condition is incompatible with life. Sometimes, organs can be donated.

Arlene Eisenberg, Heidi E. Murkoff, and Sandee E. Hathaway, *What to Expect the First Year*, 1989.

After obtaining all the necessary legal forms signed by the couple, I called the hospital administrator who, in turn, contacted the hospital attorneys. Soon I had an answer, and it was not what the family wanted to hear. There was no legal precedent to call an anencephalic baby brain dead. Accordingly, we could not transplant any organs until the baby was dead in the "official" sense of the word.

I was incredulous! "Why," I asked the lawyer, "can one of my other patients with irreversible severe damage of a previously normal brain qualify as an organ donor, but a baby with no cerebral hemispheres and only a brain stem for a brain, with an equally bleak future, cannot qualify?"

"Look, Bob," he said, "I may not agree with the law, but that's my interpretation. Don't get the hospital exposed to litigation."

The parents wished to donate the lungs, heart, kidneys, pancreas, liver and even skin, bone and bone marrow, in addition to the baby's corneas. Ultimately, the corneas would become the only parts of Laura's living tissues that would find renewed life in someone else.

Letting Her Die at Home

Since there was nothing else to do at our community hospital, I contacted two local university-affiliated medical centers that serve as regional transplantation units. They found themselves in similar legal predicaments. I was furious, and so were the parents.

However, they were not furious enough to contact their own attorney and sue to have their wishes respected, challenging the law. What they chose to do instead was to ask me if they could take Laura home and watch her die there.

I conferred with my practice associates and checked with my own attorney as well as those representing the hospital and my group corporate practice. The attorneys agreed that so long as the parents signed the necessary informed-consent forms, we could release the baby.

My partners and I visited her at home, more out of concern for the family than to provide medical expertise. The Amalfis were determined to care for their baby well, and she lived longer than any I had ever treated.

I was there, offering comfort, when she finally stopped breathing. In one of the mother's prayers that evening, she said, "Lord, let us find some day the means to heal or prevent the tragedy of anencephaly. Until then, let men and women of wisdom change the law so that families of anencephalic babies receive comfort from the knowledge that an opportunity exists to give life to others through our afflicted sons and daughters. Bless our little angel Laura and all those who have helped her and us. And bless all the children awaiting transplants, and guard over their anxious families."

Knowing of two such children with end-stage renal disease who could have profited from receiving one of Laura's kidneys, I could only express a resounding "Amen!"

"Would you feel comfortable burying this person while she is still breathing on her own? If not, you know at some level she is not dead."

Euthanizing Anencephalic Infants for Their Organs Is Unethical

J. Steven Justice

There is a huge demand for viable organs for transplant in the United States. But killing anencephalic infants to harvest their organs is not an ethical or effective way to increase the number of available organs, J. Steven Justice argues in the following viewpoint. Research shows that most anencephalic infants are not good organ donors, Justice maintains. Rather than killing living anencephalic infants, he contends, physicians should find other ways of increasing the number of viable organs. Justice, a law clerk, is a 1993 graduate of the University of Cincinnati Law School.

As you read, consider the following questions:

1. On what basis did the Florida Supreme Court decide that anencephaly cannot be equated with death, according to the author?
2. Why might ethicists oppose harvesting organs from anencephalic infants, according to Justice?
3. Why does the author support organ donation from anencephalic infants after whole brain death has occurred?

Excerpted from J. Steven Justice, "Personhood and Death—The Proper Treatment of Anencephalic Organ Donors Under the Law," *University of Cincinnati Law Review*, vol. 62, no. 3, Winter 1994. Copyright 1994 by the University of Cincinnati. Reprinted with permission.

Cultures can be judged in many ways, but eventually every nation in every age must be judged by this test: How did it treat people?
—Francis A. Schaeffer and C. Everett Koop

Doctors informed Laura Campo and Justin Pearson during Laura's eighth month of pregnancy that their child would be born with an invariably fatal birth defect called anencephaly. Infants exhibiting this condition are born with only a brainstem and otherwise lack a brain. After receiving the news of Baby Theresa's fatal birth defect and consulting with physicians, Ms. Campo and Mr. Pearson decided to carry the pregnancy to term and undergo a caesarean section because they expressly hoped that the doctors would be able to transplant Baby Theresa's functioning organs to other dying infants who had a chance to survive. The doctors believed that the caesarean section would cause less damage to Baby Theresa's organs.

Four-pound Theresa Ann Campo Pearson was born on March 21, 1992, and consistent with anencephaly, the back of her skull and upper brain were entirely missing, leaving her brainstem exposed to the air. The risk of infection was very high, so doctors wrapped her open skull in medical bandaging. Baby Theresa's heart beat spontaneously, and she could breathe unassisted at birth.

Doctors' Fears of Litigation

After her birth, the parents requested that the doctors declare Baby Theresa legally dead for the purpose of organ transplantation, but they refused. The doctors were concerned that if they "harvested" organs from a live infant, killing it in the process, they could incur civil or criminal liability under the laws of Florida. Under Florida law, Baby Theresa would not be considered legally dead until her heartbeat and respiration had ceased or her entire brain had ceased functioning. The baby's physicians and parents were also aware from similar cases that if they waited to harvest Baby Theresa's organs until she was legally dead, the organs would almost certainly be unusable.

Faced with this dilemma, the parents decided to file a petition in Florida's Broward County Circuit Court asking for a judicial declaration that the anencephalic infant was dead at birth so that her organs could be removed immediately. After hearing testimony and argument, Judge Estella Moriarty denied the request on the grounds that section 382.009(1) of the Florida Statutes did not permit Baby Theresa to be declared legally dead if the child's brainstem was functioning. The judge did hold, however, that doctors could remove the infant's nonvital organs, but none were harvested.

The parents immediately appealed to the Fourth District Court of Appeals, which upheld Judge Moriarty's ruling. The court agreed that Baby Theresa did not meet the legal definition of brain death. The parents then appealed to the Florida Supreme Court to take action in their cause, but the Supreme Court refused to hear the case until the Fourth District Court of Appeals certified that the case was of "compelling public interest." The Fourth District Court of Appeals did certify the case for immediate resolution, and the Florida Supreme Court accepted jurisdiction to resolve this case of first impression.

Baby Theresa survived only nine days after her birth. The cause of death was cardiac and respiratory failure. Although the brainstem has the capacity to control autonomic bodily functions like respiration and heartbeat, this ability soon ends when the rest of the brain is missing. When her vital organs began to fail, she was placed on a mechanical ventilator to assist her breathing, but eventually doctors removed the ventilator, and she died nineteen hours later.

International Attention

The medical evidence in the record revealed that Baby Theresa was incapable of developing any cognitive process and may have been unable to feel pain or experience sensation due to the absence of the brain cortex. The Florida Supreme Court noted, however, that this conclusion was disputed.

After careful consideration of the matter, the Florida Supreme Court unanimously concluded that it could find no basis to expand the common law to equate anencephaly with death. The court held that Florida common law recognized the cardiopulmonary definition of death, meaning that when a person's heart and breathing irreversibly ceased, she was dead. The court also held that section 382.009 of the Florida Statutes created a "whole-brain death" exception to the cardiopulmonary definition whenever artificial means were maintaining the heart and breathing. A mechanical ventilator, however, was not sustaining Baby Theresa's life at the times in question; therefore, the court used the cardiopulmonary standard to determine the question of death. In light of her spontaneous heartbeat and respiration, the court held that she was not dead under Florida common law and therefore any donation of her organs would have been illegal. Thus, the Florida Supreme Court affirmed the result of the trial court, but it did not agree with the trial court's determination that section 382.009 of the Florida Statutes, containing the "whole-brain death" standard, applied in this case.

Baby Theresa's plight drew international attention because of the medical, legal, and ethical issues involved. This was the first time a court in the United States had addressed the question of whether anencephalic infants could be considered legally dead at birth for purposes of organ donation. Not only were parents of anencephalic babies and parents whose infants needed organ transplants very interested in the court's deliberation, but the case also captured the attention of doctors, ethicists, lawyers, and virtually all people who became acquainted with it. The case implicated practical questions regarding the utility of anencephalic organ donors and the effect that the court's decision might have on organ donations in general. Lawyers wondered how the court's decision might affect the definition of death and the potential liability of doctors who performed transplant procedures on anencephalic infants. Ethicists wondered how society would prevent expansion of a special rule for anencephalic infants to other people who lacked "upper brain" capacity—for example, people in a persistent vegetative state, who might also be declared dead so that their organs could be harvested for others in need.

What Is Best?

Yet, for most observers the issue was much more basic. Here were sincere parents, trying to find some meaning and consolation in the birth of their deformed child, hoping to find that meaning through giving life to others. Other parents, whose dying infants had a chance to live if they received that needed organ transplant, longed for that rare opportunity. Finally, there was Baby Theresa. Her innocent little body was hopelessly dying. We looked at the lives and the pain, vicariously experiencing the dilemma through the actors, and we wondered what was right, what was best. . . .

In *T.A.C.P.* [the case of Theresa Ann Campo Pearson], the Supreme Court of Florida rendered a well-considered, conservative decision that upheld the dignity of all human beings. While the court did not declare any opinions on the issues it discussed, right or wrong, it did clearly elucidate the lack of consensus regarding the medical utility of using anencephalic donors and the ethical issues involved. In the absence of consensus, the court correctly concluded that it had no public necessity basis upon which to expand the common law of Florida to equate anencephaly with death. In essence, it refused to embrace a nonbiologically based understanding of personhood and thereby maintained the innate dignity and bodily integrity of all human beings.

Besides the precedent-setting nature of this decision, *T.A.C.P.* is important because it addressed the current state of this issue in three different communities: medical, ethical, and legal. Spurred by the news of a successful heart transplant in 1987 from an artificially sustained anencephalic infant, Baby Gabrielle, who had been declared brain-dead in London, Ontario, to another child at Loma Linda University in the United States, the interest in the potential use of anencephalic infants as donors grew quickly. Yet, experimentation soon proved that success was far more the exception than the norm. Interestingly, *T.A.C.P.* arose after the fervor had subsided. . . . The court's decision, coming on the heels of the previous ideological fervor, revealed not only the current absence of consensus among any of the interested communities, but it also raised the suspicion that consensus might not be achieved.

A Breathing Baby

If you were to declare anencephalic infants dead for purposes of organ donation, it would mean that you would be removing hearts from babies that breathe, suck, kick, and cry. I would need to have the individuals who passed that law feel that if it were not for organ donation they would be equally comfortable in burying a baby who was breathing, sucking, kicking, and crying.

Joyce L. Peabody in *American Medical News*, June 29, 1992.

In view of these considerations, no transplant centers in the United States are now using anencephalic infants as organ donors, or even contemplating it. They have declared an informal moratorium in the area. In London, Ontario, however, the transplant group is contemplating starting anencephalic organ donation again on a limited scale. Organ donation would only be allowed after whole brain death had occurred, congruent with current death standards in the United States.

While this approach has hardly yielded successful results in the past, it does have advantages over no experimentation. First, occasionally, an anencephalic infant will suffer whole brain death within a reasonable time after birth to allow doctors to harvest a viable organ for transplantation. The successful heart transplant from Baby Gabrielle in 1987 occurred in this manner. If the transplant programs are not functioning, even these organs will be lost and potential recipients will needlessly die.

Second, using a protocol that complies with the whole brain death standard will avoid the slippery slope ethical problems. It will not risk generally losing public confidence in transplant programs.

Third, in order to procure transplantable organs and comply with the UDDA [Uniform Determination of Death Act] standards, doctors will have to place most anencephalic infants on mechanical ventilation at birth. While this, too, possibly violates the Kantian ethic not to use a person as a means to an end, it appears to approach a better balance of all the interests involved if coupled with a reasonable time limit. . . . Use of a ventilator for a predefined length of time does prolong the dying process of the anencephalic or extend its life, depending on your perspective, but it also allows the infant to die of its own accord. In contrast, equating anencephaly with death allows a doctor to intervene and cause death through the harvesting of organs.

Working Within the Current Definition of Death

Finally, the existence of anencephalic transplant programs will serve as an incentive to develop new drugs and new techniques to maintain organ vitality until the anencephalic infant succumbs to whole brain death. Instead of falling prey to the temptation to alter the definition of death to meet the current capabilities of medical science, we should strive to improve medical science to yield better success within current definitions of death.

With an issue as fundamental to a society as the determination of life or death, it is imperative to have some sense of consensus before a change is made. While there seems to be a plethora of opinions on this issue, I close with a simple litmus test for consideration. George Annas, Professor of Health Law at Boston University, said regarding the case of Baby Theresa that

> life and death is not an individual question. In some sense, it's arbitrary, but the death line has got to be solid. The litmus test is this: Would you feel comfortable burying this person while she is still breathing on her own? If not, you know at some level she is not dead.

"The primary responsibility for making the decision of whether or not to treat a seriously ill newborn should rest with the parents of the infant."

Parents Alone Have the Right to Decide If Infant Euthanasia Is Ethical

Patricia M. Phillips

When seriously ill infants are born, decisions must be made concerning the continuation of medical treatment. In the past, parents, physicians, hospital ethics committees, and courts have all been involved in such decisions. In the following viewpoint, Patricia M. Phillips maintains that the parents' wishes concerning the treatment of a seriously ill child must be heeded. Phillips believes parents are the only ones who truly have the infant's best interests in mind. In addition, the parents are the ones who face the burdens associated with watching an infant suffer extensive medical treatment. Phillips is a contributor to *Capital University Law Review* in Columbus, Ohio.

As you read, consider the following questions:

1. What reasons does Phillips give to support her belief that physicians should not be solely responsible for treatment decisions for seriously ill newborns?
2. How does the "right of privacy" relate to the decision to treat a seriously ill newborn, in the author's opinion?

Excerpted from Patricia M. Phillips, "Treatment Decisions for Seriously Ill Newborns: Who Should Decide?" originally published in *Capital University Law Review*, vol. 21 (1992):219-62. Reprinted with permission.

Imagine becoming the proud parents of a newborn child—a child that one has anticipated for months, or sometimes, even years. This child may be the manifestation of one's declaration that life is good and worthy of continuation. This child may be the physical embodiment of one's dreams, one's aspirations, and one's hopes for the future.

Then imagine the devastation that one must feel when informed by health care personnel that the child is seriously impaired, mentally and/or physically, with such anomalies as myelomeningocele [exposed spinal cord], anencephaly [partial or total absence of the brain], trisomy 21 [Down's syndrome], or trisomy 13 [a chromosomal abnormality resulting in heart defects and other problems]. Decisions must be made regarding whether to treat these life threatening conditions, or to withhold treatment and let the child die. . . .

Who Should Decide?

The challenge of deciding what course of action to follow under these circumstances can be most devastating and tormenting for all concerned, including parents of these seriously ill infants, physicians either associated with the child's birth or with the ensuing surgical and medical intervention, the legal community, and society in general. However tormenting and difficult the decision may be, it must be made. At present, these decisions are being made by a variety of entities. Sometimes parents make the decision, sometimes physicians decide, and sometimes judicial intervention is requested by parents or physicians when the judgment of an objective decision maker is desired. In some instances, legislative action and judicial decisions have overridden parental decisions not to treat their seriously ill child. . . .

It is my conclusion that the primary responsibility for making the decision of whether or not to treat a seriously ill newborn should rest with the parents of the infant, but only after the parent has consulted with the infant's physician. This decision is not a legal decision in the traditional sense, which ordinarily lends itself to resolution by the adversarial process, or to legislative pronouncements. However, the decision is a legal decision, to the extent that it involves the individual rights of privacy and autonomy of both parents and infants. Such rights have been enunciated by various courts in the making of just this type of decision.

Since the family must live with the consequence of any decision made with regard to sustaining or withholding treatment, it is imperative that the decision ultimately is left to the parents. Neither physicians, hospital infant care review committees, nor the legal system should be permitted to usurp the fundamental right that abides in parents to make important decisions with regard to what is best for the children they have brought into existence. . . .

A. Physicians. Various legal and medical commentators have considered whether physicians should make the decision to sustain or withhold treatment from seriously ill newborns. Physicians would possess the requisite medical information necessary to render an informed decision, if the decision is based on a thorough diagnosis of the severity of the infant's defects, and the anticipated prognosis regarding future medical developments. . . . Physicians can quickly assess the infant's chances for survival without treatment, and the prognosis for future health and quality of life if treatment is afforded. . . .

However well trained, objective, and experienced the physician may be when confronted with these profoundly important life and death decisions, there are many factors militating against relegating the decision to the physician. Medical school training urges physicians to view medicine as a battle against death; therefore, physicians are reluctant to discuss or even consider nontreatment as an option, even when the parents have indicated that they think treatment should be withheld. Physicians often feel that to "give up" and to render no treatment is disloyal to the medical profession. Some physicians only want the parents' cooperation when the physicians apply their knowledge and skills in making a decision, even if the parents are not always grateful. These attitudes indicate that some physicians do not fully understand the complexity surrounding the decision of whether or not to treat these infants. Physicians view the decision in medical terms only. Their only concern is with the scientific, biological processes of life, not with the moral, ethical, financial or religious concerns that must be considered when decisions of this magnitude must be made. . . .

The Physician's Personal Views

Another argument against allowing physicians to make treatment decisions for seriously ill newborns is that physicians have their own moral perceptions regarding the consequences of treating or foregoing treatment. Since the consequences of the decision ultimately amount to life or death, the physician may be influenced by her own personal, religious, moral, or ethical views regarding quality of life, considerations of the societal value of the life of a handicapped child, and other factors that are clearly outside the physician's medical expertise. These factors may greatly influence the physician's advice to the parents when discussing treatment alternatives. The physician may harbor feelings of guilt or failure. . . . If the decision is to be wrested from the parents and placed in the hands of the physician, there is a great risk that the decision will be made, not with the parents or the infant's best interests in mind, but with the physician's interests, biases, prejudices, and paternalistic urges as the controlling factors in the decision-making process. . . .

B. Parents. In the preceding section, I argued that physicians should not be afforded unfettered discretion in the decision-making process regarding treatment for seriously ill newborns. Another solution to the dilemma of who should be the primary decision maker in these seriously ill newborn cases centers around the infant's parents and family. There are many arguments that can be made for and against parental decision making. I . . . conclude that under all disciplines—the law, ethics, and morality—the parents should be the primary decision-making body, unencumbered by either the medical community or the legal system. . . .

The Right of Privacy

A most basic and fundamental argument for allowing parents to choose whether to sustain or withhold treatment from their seriously ill newborn is found in the "right of privacy", or the "right to be left alone", [as found in U.S. Supreme Court cases *Olmstead v. United States, California v. Ciraolo, F.C.C. v. Pacifica Foundation,* and *Carey v. Brown*]. Although the United States Constitution does not explicitly mention a "right of privacy", this right has been found to exist in the First, Fourth, Fifth, Ninth, and Fourteenth Amendments. The privacy right has at times been referred to as an "interest in independence in making certain kinds of important decisions" [as in *Whalen v. Roe*]. Furthermore, the right of privacy has been held in many judicial decisions to include freedom of choice in marital decisions and decisions regarding contraception and child bearing. The decision of whether to sustain or withhold treatment from a seriously ill newborn clearly encompasses the very essence of what the right to privacy protects. Deciding to withhold treatment from or compel treatment for an ill child is undeniably one of the most important decisions a parent could ever be forced to make. Certainly the right to make this decision in private, without the burden of state intervention, is encompassed in the language used by the Supreme Court. If a potential parent possesses a right of privacy to choose to terminate a pregnancy that may result in a completely normal, high functioning, intelligent, healthy human being, then it follows that this same right of privacy should be extended to a parent faced with the decision of whether to sustain or withhold treatment from an infant who would exist with minimal cognitive functioning, little, if any interaction with other human beings, and who would live a life of extreme pain and suffering. . . .

A value that parents of seriously ill newborns may legitimately consider when weighing treatment options is one that takes into account the pain and suffering that must be endured by the infant if treatment is given. The parents may determine that this suffering constitutes cruel and inhumane treatment of their child, and, using their own religious, moral and philosophical values, may conclude that this prolongation of suffering is morally, religiously, and ethically not within their child's best interests. In making treatment decisions parents must be afforded the autonomy, privacy, intimacy, and freedom to make these decisions based on their own deeply held values, free from unwarranted, aggressive intrusions into the decision-making process.

Some Severe Impairments of Newborns

Condition	Description
Myelomeningocele	Commonly called spina bifida cystica. One of the most common of the severe anomalies in newborns. Infants suffering from this condition may have malformed and exposed spinal cords, which typically results in lower extremity paralysis and lack of bladder and bowel control and enlargement of the head caused by excess fluid in the skull. Mental impairment occurs often in these infants. Without surgical or medical intervention to close the skin defect and drain excess fluid from the brain, infants with this condition usually die within days or months.
Trisomy 21	Commonly called Down's syndrome. A condition characterized by a chromosomal abnormality, which produces varying degrees of mental retardation. Expectations are of an IQ of 60 at best. This condition is often accompanied by serious bowel and heart defects, which usually require surgical intervention to save the infant's life.
Trisomy 13	A chromosomal abnormality that occurs in about one out of every five thousand births. The condition results in serious heart defects and bowel abnormalities, blindness, cataracts, profound retardation, deafness, and serious deformities of the limbs. Infants with this condition may require respirators, pacemakers, and intravenous feeding. Death usually occurs within three months, if no surgical intervention is afforded.

Adapted from Patricia M. Phillips, *Capital University Law Review*, vol. 21, no. 219, 1992.

Although intruders often purport to act in the best interest of the child, they really have no conception of the devastating pain and sorrow these parents endure when making these types of decisions. Parents deserve the protection afforded by the right of privacy to make treatment decisions for their children. . . .

The Importance of Family Autonomy

The major emphasis on family or parental autonomy in decision making arises from the theory that infants, and most especially infants that are severely and permanently medically and physically impaired, are not "self directing or self defining beings," as Phoebe Haddon has noted, and, therefore, have no existence outside of the domain of the family unit. These infants are considered persons only in a social sense and, therefore, possess the potential to develop only if they are provided nourishment, care, love, and support by parents and other family members. Parents hold the rights and duties of these potential persons in trust until the infant has fulfilled his or her potential and can repossess these rights and duties from the parents. This conception of family autonomy suggests that in order to respect a newborn's privacy interest in making medical treatment decisions, one must honor the parents, as substitute decision makers, in any decision made on behalf of the infant. This construction of family autonomy squarely places the decision to sustain or withhold treatment with the parents, as the exclusive agents for determining the child's best interest. The parents are undeniably in the best position to determine what is best for their child, within their family unit, at this juncture of the family's development. If the child exists only within the familial boundaries and has no existence as an individual being, then clearly the parents are the only persons capable of making the determination of how this child's existence will affect the familial setting into which he or she is born. . . .

In addition to the legal arguments for allowing parents to be the primary decision makers in these treatment dilemmas, there are also moral and ethical considerations that point toward the parent as the principal decision maker. Parents must ask themselves what consequences will follow from a decision to sustain or withhold treatment. The parents are concerned with quality of life considerations, how much pain and suffering the child will endure, and whether treatment will actually be in the child's best interest. No other societal group involved in the decision-making process—not physicians, not courts, not the legislature—must live first hand with the consequences of the decision. The physician can make her medical evaluation and assessment of the infant's prognosis, the legislature can promulgate rules mandating treatment, and the courts can affirm or overrule decisions that have already been made. But none of these outside groups will agonize over the consequences of the decision in quite the way the parents will.

Parents Are Morally Accountable

As the decision to sustain or withhold treatment ultimately ends or preserves the life of the infant, the parental role should be primary in the making of these decisions. Parents are morally accountable for the decision because of the close relationship between parent and child. Parents of any child are the closest to understanding whatever is capable of being understood about the child's life as a human being. No one is more intensely focused on the child's well-being than the parents. In the infant's short existence, parents have been the only source of human connection. A profound interest in the child, and in the child's welfare and best interest, is exhibited by no one quite as intensely as that exhibited by the child's parents. It is unreasonable and unfair to perceive parents as being completely self-motivated when faced with these treatment dilemmas. If the parent is properly informed by medical personnel of all consequences of any treatment decision, the parent's decision to sustain or withhold treatment should be accepted by both the medical community and the legal community. . . .

Currently, there is little consistency in the process by which treatment decisions are made for infants who are considered to be seriously impaired. . . . The resolution of issues presented in this viewpoint is of utmost importance in today's world of ultra modern medical technology. Because the decision to treat or withhold treatment from a seriously ill newborn is fraught with complex moral, ethical, social, and psychological dilemmas, the decision must not be relegated to any societal group that has no profound interest in its outcome. Physicians, infant care review committees, and the legal system have no personal, moral, or philosophical interest in these treatment decisions. There are some areas into which the law should not tread. Medical treatment decisions for seriously ill newborns is one such area. It is exceptionally difficult to formulate any substantive guidelines for decision making in the area of treatment for seriously ill newborns. Therefore, as the parents are truly the only persons that stand to be affected by the consequences of these decisions in the most personal, private, and profound way imaginable, it is imperative that these decisions be left to their judgment. Parents, in close consultation with medical, spiritual, and ethical advisors, should be afforded the right and responsibility to make these determinations free from any intrusive, unwarranted outside intervention.

"Emotional distress, . . . fear of raising an impaired child, . . . [and] 'idiosyncratic' views . . . may interfere with a parent's ability to determine a child's best interests."

Parents Should Not Decide Alone If Infant Euthanasia Is Ethical

Jennifer Stokley

It is difficult to decide whether an extremely premature new-born should receive medical treatment or not. This decision and its ramifications are too great to be made by the parents alone, Jennifer Stokley states in the following viewpoint. The parents, physicians, hospital ethics committees, and the courts all have a role to play in deciding how or if to treat a premature newborn, she argues. If all of these groups are involved, there is a greater chance that the ultimate decision will be in the best interests of the infant. Stokley is a third-year law student at the University of North Dakota and editor in chief of the school's law review.

As you read, consider the following questions:

1. According to Stokley, why are more doctors choosing to aggressively treat premature newborns, even if there is little hope for survival?
2. What biases might cause hospital ethics committees to make poor decisions concerning treatment, in the author's opinion?
3. What three criticisms of federal involvement in medical decision making does the author cite?

Excerpted from Jennifer Stokley, "Withdrawing or Withholding Medical Care from Premature Infants: Who Should Decide, and How?" *North Dakota Law Review*, vol. 70, no. 1, 1994. Reprinted with permission.

A young woman arrives at a hospital in labor. She is at approximately twenty-six weeks gestation. She is poor and has had no prenatal care. She has a history of cocaine use. The infant is born weighing less than 750 grams. A neonatologist takes over. She wonders if the infant is viable. The child has difficulty breathing, and his heart rate is too fast. The doctor is not optimistic, but she wants to give the infant a chance. She inserts a breathing tube in the infant's airway and begins artificial ventilation. The infant is transported to a tertiary care facility and admitted to a neonatal intensive care unit [hereinafter NICU], where he is placed on a respirator.

Brain Damage and Infection

Six weeks later, the infant remains in the NICU. Because he is still dependent on the respirator, he has developed a chronic lung disease. A heart defect related to prematurity has failed to correct itself, which has exacerbated the lung problem. The infant also exhibits signs of considerable brain damage due to his prematurity. In addition, he has developed a severe bowel infection common among premature infants.

The infant's prognosis is uncertain. Surgery will be necessary to assess the damage to his digestive tract. Dead bowel tissue must be removed, and if too much is removed for the infant to digest food, he will never be able to eat orally and will die within a few years. In addition, he may live with severe neurosensory handicaps due to brain damage. He may remain hospitalized and dependent on life-support machines for the rest of his life. Or, he may die very soon as a result of the bowel condition, the severe brain damage, or the lung disease. Meanwhile, he is isolated, dependent on machines for his basic functions, and regularly subjected to invasive procedures which may cause him pain. His mother has decided that she wants aggressive medical treatment to be withdrawn and resuscitative measures to be withheld. What now? This hypothetical case illustrates some of the medical difficulties encountered with premature infants and some of the reasons that medical decision-making in such cases is difficult.

The care of very premature infants has become one of the major frontiers of medicine. By the 1920s, physicians realized that the birth process merited medical attention, and hospital births gradually became standard. The problems of premature births received little attention, however, until the 1960s. During and after that decade, breakthroughs came about in ventilation and nutrition for premature infants, NICUs multiplied, and many more doctors specialized in neonatal practice and research. In recent years, slightly less than two percent of all births in the United States have been very premature (under 32 weeks gestation). As *Taber's Cyclopedic Medical Dictionary* states, "Prematurity is the leading cause of death in the neonatal period" and complications related to prematurity "vary in direct proportion to the degree of immaturity present."

Doctors' Decisions

Ethical dilemmas in the treatment of these infants are first confronted at the time of delivery because "no clear guidelines dictate the initial delivery room care of the extremely immature infant (<750 g)," according to Maureen Hack and Avroy A. Fanaroff. The physician must decide whether, and how aggressively, to treat the infant. This decision is complicated by the immediacy of the situation and by the presence of other persons under stress. It is further complicated by the difficult assessment of whether or not the infant is viable. In practice, more and more doctors are initially providing aggressive treatment in all but the worst cases. While doctors do not want to begin treatment that will prove futile, they are even more wary of a delay in treatment that will harm an infant who does survive. Because of the enormous uncertainty about prognosis at delivery, doctors also want to buy time with which to gather more information.

For the parents and doctors of premature infants who survive but do not improve, uncertainty may be prolonged considerably. The situation is further complicated by the fact that the very treatments which such infants need to survive may also be harmful. Parents and doctors in such cases may contemplate withdrawal of certain treatments or withholding of resuscitative measures. The ethical and legal issues are difficult and unique. . . .

Parents and Physicians

A. Parents. Physicians have recognized the importance of the parental role in making treatment decisions for infants, particularly premature infants whose cases are often uncertain. Courts also have recognized the advisability of giving parents the primary role in decisions to withhold or withdraw care from infants. However, commentators have argued for limits to parental discretion. Emotional distress at the premature birth of a child may be overwhelming, and parental ability to make sound decisions may initially be impaired. Fear of raising an impaired child may influence decisions, as may individual biases of parents about such children. Finally, some parents may harbor "idiosyncratic" views such as a fear of technology or a moral bias against blood transfusions. All of these factors may interfere with a parent's ability to determine a child's best interests.

B. Physicians. Physicians may have biases of their own which may interfere with an objective best interests analysis in some cases. A bias toward nontreatment in marginal cases may cause a physician not to recommend aggressive treatments. On the other hand, some doctors may have a bias toward aggressive treatment for a number of reasons. As one observer of an NICU, Fred M. Frohock, relates, "[m]any of the sickest babies in the nursery appeal to the doctors' self-image as crisis managers." Doctors also may favor aggressive treatment in order to obtain research funding, practice treatment techniques, or instruct junior physicians. They may wish to further the reputation of the hospital as a research center or a facility with high survival statistics for very premature infants. They also may be influenced by personal moral judgments. In some cases, doctors may cross the fine line between conventional and experimental treatments. Whether a doctor provides less aggressive or more aggressive treatment, problems can arise in communication with parents. The physician usually has an authoritative position vis-à-vis the parents in discussions of treatment options and may present options with a slanted view. Communication also may be less effective if doctors are uncertain about the medical situation or if they do not provide parents with enough information because of delicacy, time constraints, or a lack of appreciation of the wide gap between the parents' understanding and their own. In such cases, parental consent may not be truly informed. Physician William A. Silverman illustrates these problems in describing an experience that occurred with a premature infant with whom he had tried experimental procedures:

> The baby was presented at grand rounds as a triumph of mechanism-guided treatment, and I was made to feel like a hero. My rescue fantasy was fulfilled.
>
> I was very disappointed that the parents did not share these joyous feelings of high adventure. . . . They were completely overwhelmed by what I was doing to prolong the life of this . . . baby. I tried to focus their attention on the miraculous present, and I was annoyed that their thoughts were fixed on an uncertain future. They kept asking about long-term outlook. I was forced to admit I had no idea about prognosis because few, if any, infants of this size ever survived. . . .
>
> As I take a long look back at this experience, I see that the moral judgment of these parents was much more highly developed than mine.

C. Hospital Ethics Committees. Many hospitals, particularly tertiary care centers, have developed internal ethics committees to provide guidance and/or review for difficult treatment decisions. An ethics committee may be made up of physicians, nurses, attorneys, clergy members, medical ethicists, hospital administrators, and community members. While few courts have critiqued the role of ethics committees in treatment decisions for incompetent patients, commentators have noted benefits, as well as problems, with committee involvement.

On the one hand, ethics committees may provide expedited, flexible, and objective review in a nonadversarial setting. They may promote consistency in the decision-making process. They also may ensure that community values are incorporated into the process. Committees can provide additional expertise from doctors and nurses not directly involved with the patient and a forum for full, interdisciplinary discussion of treatment options. This may help to counter any individual physician biases. Committee involvement may facilitate communication between the parents and the attending physician, which may lessen the intimidation that parents may feel in dealing with a physician. The committee can ensure that parents are fully informed about the medical facts and that they are making a rational decision rather than an emotional one. Finally, review and guidance from an ethics committee may prevent judicial involvement.

The Physician's Responsibility

It is important to understand that the child is the patient and the physician is the physician to the child. If, in the opinion of the physician, the parents are advocating treatment that is not in the child's best interest, the physician must ethically act in accordance with his own perception of what is best for the child.

David G. McLone, *Issues in Law & Medicine*, vol. 2, no. 1, Winter 1986.

However, commentators also have noted disadvantages and dangers of ethics committee involvement in treatment decision-making. A committee may make unsatisfactory compromises to achieve consensus, and it may inappropriately diffuse decision-making responsibility. Physicians on the committee may only serve to reinforce biases of the treating physician, and members may be motivated by institutional biases. If a committee with nonphysician members has a great deal of influence over treatment decisions, it may venture into the unlicensed practice of medicine. In addition, privacy and confidentiality for patients and families may be jeopardized if nonmedical and even noninstitutional committee members learn the details of each case.

Some of these potential dangers may be avoided by making committee review optional and subject to parental consent. Legal limitations on committee authority and a guarantee of parental access to committee records may be advisable. Commentators also have argued that ethics committees should "work from clearly articulated principles and guidelines." In addition, committees may benefit from the membership of parents of handicapped children who can provide a perspective on the results of treatment decisions.

D. Judicial Involvement. Commentators have noted that routine judicial involvement may be ill-suited to treatment decisions for premature infants for several reasons. First, the courts are not able to respond quickly enough or knowledgeably enough to these unique, complex, and rapidly changing medical situations. Furthermore, litigation may involve additional stress for parents and physicians alike and may sacrifice family privacy. The cost of counsel often will be prohibitive for parents who already face huge medical bills. Finally, one commentator has argued that requiring judicial approval only for nontreatment decisions sends parents the message that consenting to aggressive treatment is the path of least resistance.

Court Decisions

Several courts have agreed that routine judicial oversight of decisions to withhold or withdraw treatment from incompetent persons would be inappropriate. However, these decisions indicated that courts remained open to hear such cases if needed. Other courts have agreed that judicial involvement is not necessary in all cases but have carefully limited that policy. Finally, some courts have expressed a judicial preference for court approval in all cases of withdrawal of treatment from incompetent persons.

E. Governmental Involvement. Federal involvement in medical decision-making for infants has been criticized for practical reasons. Congress and federal agencies are prone to compromise and to pressure from special interests. Also, Congress and federal agencies are ill-equipped to mandate narrow policies in such a complex and uncertain area of medicine. Federal policies may threaten state constitutional protections as well.

State governmental involvement may be criticized for some of the same reasons, but some commentators have suggested that state statutes which specifically address withholding or withdrawal of medical treatment from minors and infants would be helpful. The child abuse and neglect statutes of most states may be inapplicable to such situations or may not deal with them adequately. On the other hand, statutes which deal with withdrawal of care from adults may not take into account the roles of the child and its parents. Courts in recent years have requested state legislatures to take action in this area.

The Infant's Best Interests

Should the infant in our hypothetical case receive surgery? Should his ventilator treatment be continued, and if so, for how long? In making these decisions, all parties involved should focus upon the best interests of the infant. . . . To ascertain the infant's best interests, the benefits of treatment should be weighed against the probable burdens. This balancing test necessarily involves quality of life considerations because benefits and burdens are defined qualitatively from the infant's perspective.

In our hypothetical case, the infant's mother wants surgery withheld and ventilator treatment withdrawn. As a parent presumed to act in her child's best interests, she should have a primary role in making such decisions. However, the mother's discretion should not be unchecked. Doctors should ensure that she is making informed and rational decisions based upon the child's best interests in light of the medical prognosis, and not based upon fear or bewilderment. On the other hand, the doctors' discretion should also be checked. A hospital ethics committee should ensure that the doctors, too, are motivated by the child's best interests. If the doctors agree with the mother that treatment should be withdrawn or withheld, the ethics committee should perform this checking function merely by reviewing the medical facts and determining whether the decision to withhold or withdraw treatment is reasonable in light of those facts. If doctors disagree with the mother or among themselves, the ethics committee should play the role of a mediator, taking a more active role to facilitate communication between the parties and to ensure that all parties are using appropriate decision-making standards. If this process works, judicial intervention should not be necessary. If the court must get involved, then it, like the ethics committee, should first act as a mediator. If the court must decide whether treatment should be withdrawn or withheld, then it, too, should employ the best interests standard and weigh the benefits of treatment against the burdens.

Following these guidelines will not produce an ideal result for this infant or for his mother. The most that can be hoped for is that the mother and the doctors will make informed treatment decisions in light of the infant's best interests. This standard may at least prevent withdrawal of treatment too hastily. It may also prevent continuation of treatment for too long.

Periodical Bibliography

The following articles have been selected to supplement the diverse views presented in this chapter.

Dave Andrusko | "Anencephalic Babies Not 'Dead,' Court Rules," *National Right to Life News*, December 14, 1992. Available from 419 Seventh St. NW, Suite 500, Washington, DC 20004.

Jeffrey R. Botkin | "Delivery Room Decisions for Tiny Infants: An Ethical Analysis," *Journal of Clinical Ethics*, Winter 1990. Available from 107 E. Church St., Frederick, MD 21701.

Paul A. Byrne, Joseph C. Evers, and Richard G. Nilges | "Anencephaly—Organ Transplantation," *Issues in Law & Medicine*, Summer 1993. Available from Box 1586, Terre Haute, IN 47808-1586.

Frank I. Clark | "Withdrawal of Life-Support in the Newborn: Whose Baby Is It?" *Southwestern University Law Review*, vol. 23, no. 1, 1993. Available from Southwestern University School of Law, 675 S. Westmoreland Ave., Los Angeles, CA 90005.

Henk Jochemsen | "Life-Prolonging and Life-Terminating Treatment for Severely Handicapped Newborn Babies," *Issues in Law & Medicine*, Fall 1992.

Julie Koenig | "The Anencephalic Baby Theresa: A Prognosticator of Future Bioethics," *Nova Law Review*, vol. 17, Fall 1992. Available from Shepard Broad Law Center, 3305 College Ave., Fort Lauderdale, FL 33314.

Carole Outterson | "A Report from the United Kingdom: Newborn Infants with Severe Defects," *Bioethics*, October 1993. Available from Basil Blackwell, 238 Main St., Suite 501, Cambridge, MA 02142.

Karoly Schultz | "Hungarian Paediatricians' Attitudes Regarding the Treatment and Non-treatment of Defective Newborns, a Comparative Study," *Bioethics*, January 1993.

Bonnie P. Tucker | "The U.S. Civil Rights Commission Report, 'Medical Discrimination Against Children with Disabilities': A Brief Commentary," *Issues in Law & Medicine*, Winter 1990.

For Further Discussion

Chapter 1

1. Derek Humphry, the author of Viewpoint 1, helped his terminally ill first wife commit suicide. How does knowing this about him affect your assessment of his viewpoint? Does his personal experience make his opinion more credible than Ronald Otremba's? Explain your answer.

2. Ronald Dworkin writes that decisions about euthanasia must be made by individuals, not by governmental authorities. Is euthanasia a personal decision, or do society and the government have some right to regulate such decisions? Defend your answer.

3. Explain J. David Bleich's and Joseph Edelheit's views on the relationship between euthanasia and the will of God. In your view, is a discussion of God's will appropriate and/or necessary when considering the ethical nature of euthanasia? Explain your answer.

Chapter 2

1. Both Edward J. Larson and Jack Lessenberry discuss the role of personal autonomy in the euthanasia debate. How do their views concerning the importance of personal autonomy differ? Which author's view is more persuasive? Why?

2. Charles J. Dougherty and John A. Pridonoff both state that public opinion concerning the morality of euthanasia can change quickly. Dougherty fears this change in opinion, while Pridonoff welcomes it. Explain their reasons for their different views. Which author do you agree with? Why?

3. Opponents of legalized euthanasia fear that it will lead to involuntary euthanasia, especially of the weak in society. How do Lawrence J. Schneiderman and his colleagues refute this argument? Do you think the fears of such opponents are justified? Why or why not?

Chapter 3

1. Why does David Cundiff believe physician-assisted suicide is unnecessary? How do Theresa M. Stephany's views differ from Cundiff's? What would be your opinion concerning physician-assisted suicide if you were (a) a physician; (b) a terminally ill patient; (c) a family member of a terminally ill patient?

2. What fears does Edmund D. Pellegrino have concerning physician-assisted suicide? What safeguards do Franklin G. Miller and his colleagues believe could assuage such fears? Do you think such safeguards would be effective? Explain your response.

3. The Hippocratic oath is the traditional oath made by physicians. In it, physicians promise never to injure or harm their patients. In your view, is physician-assisted suicide contrary to or in keeping with the oath? Explain your answer.

Chapter 4

1. William McCord and Daniel Callahan have opposing views concerning the difference between withholding treatment and assisting in suicide. What are their respective opinions? Which author is the more persuasive, and why?

2. David F. Kelly argues that the family should be allowed to help make decisions about euthanasia. What benefits and problems do you foresee if a patient's family had the right to make such decisions?

3. Explain Daniel Callahan's view. Do you find his arguments persuasive? Why or why not? Callahan is a noted bioethicist. How does knowing this fact change your opinion of his views, if at all?

Chapter 5

1. How do Robert J. Lerer and J. Steven Justice differ in their views on how to protect the dignity of anencephalic newborns? If you were the parent of an anencephalic newborn, would you choose euthanasia for the infant so that its organs could be donated? Why or why not?

2. How do Patricia M. Phillips and Jennifer Stokley differ in their views on the extent of parental rights in cases of severely handicapped newborns? Explain each of their views. Which author is more persuasive? Did either author affect your views on whether parents should make decisions for their children? If so, how?

3. Who do you believe should be responsible for determining if a severely handicapped newborn will be treated or not—parents? physicians? hospital ethics committees? the courts? or all of these parties? Explain your view. Discuss the possible benefits and pitfalls if each of these groups were given sole power to make the decision to euthanize infants.

Organizations to Contact

The editors have compiled the following list of organizations concerned with the issues debated in this book. The descriptions are derived from materials provided by the organizations. All have publications or information available for interested readers. The list was compiled on the date of publication of the present volume; names, addresses, and phone numbers may change. Be aware that many organizations take several weeks or longer to respond to inquiries, so allow as much time as possible.

American Life League (ALL)
PO Box 1350
Stafford, VA 22554
(703) 659-4171
fax: (703) 659-2586

ALL is a pro-life organization that provides information and educational materials to organizations opposed to physician-assisted suicide and abortion. Its publications include pamphlets, reports, the monthly newsletter *ALL About Issues,* and books such as *Choice in Matters of Life and Death* and *The Living Will.*

American Medical Association (AMA)
515 N. State St.
Chicago, IL 60610
(312) 464-4818
fax: (312) 464-4184

The AMA is the primary professional association of physicians in the United States. Founded in 1847, it disseminates information to its members and the public concerning medical breakthroughs, medical and health legislation, educational standards for physicians, and other issues concerning medicine and health care. It opposes physician-assisted suicide. The AMA operates a library and offers many publications, including its weekly journal, *JAMA,* the weekly newspaper *American Medical News,* and journals covering specific types of medical specialties.

American Society of Law, Medicine, and Ethics
765 Commonwealth Ave., Suite 1634
Boston, MA 02215
(617) 262-4990
fax: (617) 437-7596

The society's members include physicians, attorneys, health care administrators, and others interested in the relationship between law, medicine, and ethics. It takes no positions, but acts as a forum for discussion of issues such as euthanasia and assisted suicide. The organization has an information clearinghouse and a library. It publishes the quarterlies *American Journal of Law and Medicine* and *Journal of Law, Medicine, and Ethics,* the periodic *ASLM Briefings,* and books such as *Legal and Ethical Aspects of Treating Critically and Terminally Ill Patients.*

Americans United for Life (AUL)
343 S. Dearborn St., Suite 1804
Chicago, IL 60604
(312) 786-9494

AUL is committed to promoting public awareness of the sacredness of all human life, including the lives of fetuses, handicapped newborns, the elderly, and comatose patients. It lobbies against the legalization of euthanasia. It publishes several books and essays on euthanasia, the monthly *AUL Forum*, and a newsletter.

Association for Retarded Citizens of the United States
500 E. Border St., Suite 300
Arlington, TX 76010
(817) 261-6003
fax: (817) 277-3491

The association works to preserve the rights of mentally retarded citizens of all ages. It adopted a resolution in 1986 opposing the withdrawal of food and water from mentally retarded infants. The association publishes monthly and bimonthly newsletters and distributes books and pamphlets.

Center for Biomedical Ethics
3-110 Owre Hall
UMHC Box 33
Harvard St. and E. River Rd.
Minneapolis, MN 55455

The center studies the ethical implications of biomedical practices such as euthanasia, physician-assisted suicide, organ transplantation, and fetal tissue research. It publishes reading packets that provide introductory overviews to specific topics. Each packet includes a discussion of the topic's central issues, articles, a bibliography, additional reading materials, and a forecast of future debate on the topic. Packet titles include *Withholding or Withdrawing Artificial Nutrition and Hydration*, *Termination of Treatment of Adults*, and *Individual Responsibility for Health*. In addition, the center publishes articles, books, and reports.

Center for the Rights of the Terminally Ill
PO Box 54246
Hurst, TX 76054-2064
(817) 656-5143

The center opposes euthanasia and assisted suicide and works to protect the rights of the elderly, handicapped, sick, and dying. It believes legalized euthanasia would threaten these groups. The center provides educational materials and programs. Its publications include pamphlets such as *Living Wills: Unnecessary, Counterproductive, Dangerous* and *Can Cancer Pain Be Relieved?*

Choice in Dying—The National Council for the Right to Die
200 Varick St., 10th Fl.
New York, NY 10014-4810
(212) 366-5540
(800) 989-WILL
fax: (212) 366-5337

Choice in Dying educates professionals and the public on the legal, ethical, and psychological consequences of decisions concerning the terminally ill. For example, it provides physicians with information about the consequences of assisting in a patient's suicide or taking part in euthanasia. The council publishes booklets and the quarterly *Choice in Dying News* and distributes living will documents.

Disability Rights Education and Defense Fund
2212 Sixth St.
Berkeley, CA 94710
(510) 644-2555
fax: (510) 841-8645

This organization works to further the civil rights and liberties of the disabled. It opposes infant euthanasia. The fund maintains a Disability Law National Support Center that identifies key disability issues. It publishes books and the quarterly *Disability Rights News*.

The Hastings Center
255 Elm Rd.
Briarcliff Manor, NY 10510
(914) 762-8500
fax: (914) 762-2124

Since its founding in 1969, the center has played a central role in responding to advances in medicine, the biological sciences, and the social sciences by raising ethical questions related to such advances. It conducts research and provides consultations on ethical issues. It does not take a position on issues such as euthanasia and assisted suicide but offers a forum for exploration and debate. The center publishes books, papers, guidelines, and the bimonthly *Hastings Center Report*.

The Hemlock Society
PO Box 11830
Eugene, OR 97440-3900
(503) 342-5748
(800) 247-7421
fax: (503) 345-2751

The society believes that terminally ill individuals have the right to commit suicide. It supports the practice of voluntary suicide and physician-assisted suicide for the terminally ill. The society publishes books on suicide, death, and dying, including *Final Exit*, a guide to those suffering with terminal illness and considering suicide. The society also publishes the *Hemlock Quarterly*.

Human Life International (HLI)
7845 Airpark Rd., Suite E
Gaithersburg, MD 20879
(301) 670-7884
fax: (301) 869-7363

The pro-life Human Life International is a research, educational, and service organization. It opposes euthanasia, infant euthanasia, and assisted suicide. The group publishes books such as *Death Without Dignity*, pamphlets, and the monthly *HLI Reports*.

National Hospice Organization
1901 N. Moore St., Suite 901
Arlington, VA 22209
(703) 243-5900
(800) 658-8898
fax: (703) 525-5762

The organization works to educate the public about the benefits of hospice care for the terminally ill and their families. It seeks to promote the idea that with the proper care and pain medication, the terminally ill can live out their lives comfortably and in the company of their families. The organization opposes euthanasia and assisted suicide. It conducts educational and training programs for administrators and caregivers in numerous aspects of hospice care. It publishes the quarterlies *Hospice Journal* and *Hospice Magazine* as well as books and monographs.

National Right to Life
419 Seventh St. NW, Suite 500
Washington, DC 20004-2293
(202) 626-8800
fax: (202) 737-9189

National Right to Life opposes euthanasia, physician-assisted suicide, and abortion because it believes these practices disregard the value of human life. The group organizes protests at the national and local level and publishes many articles, pamphlets, and reports to promote its position. Its *National Right to Life News* is published twice a month.

Park Ridge Center
211 E. Ontario, Suite 800
Chicago, IL 60611-3215
(312) 266-2222
fax: (312) 266-6068

The Park Ridge Center explores the relationship between the issues of health care, religious faith, and ethics. It is a forum for discussion and debate about topics such as euthanasia and assisted suicide. The center publishes monographs, including *Active Euthanasia, Religion, and the Public Debate*, and the quarterly journal *Second Opinion*.

Bibliography of Books

Michael Betzold   *Appointment with Doctor Death.* Troy, MI: Momentum Books, 1993.

George M. Burnell   *Final Choices: To Live or to Die in an Age of Medical Technology.* New York: Plenum Press, 1993.

Donald W. Cox   *Hemlock's Cup: The Struggle for Death with Dignity.* Buffalo: Prometheus Books, 1993.

David Cundiff   *Euthanasia Is Not the Answer: A Hospice Physician's View.* Totowa, NJ: Humana Press, 1992.

Eileen Doyle   *A Pro-Life Primer on Euthanasia.* Stafford, VA: American Life Lobby, 1985.

Ronald Dworkin   *Life's Dominion: An Argument About Abortion, Euthanasia, and Individual Freedom.* New York: Knopf, 1993.

Luke Gormally, ed.   *Euthanasia, Clinical Practice, and the Law.* Indianapolis: Hacket Publishing Co., 1994.

Jeanne Harley Guillemin and Lynda Lytle Holmstrom   *Mixed Blessings: Intensive Care for Newborns.* New York: Oxford University Press, 1986.

Rasa Gustaitis and Ernle W.D. Young   *A Time to Be Born, a Time to Die.* Reading, MA: Addison-Wesley, 1986.

Ron Hamel, ed.,   *Choosing Death: Active Euthanasia: Religion, and the Public Debate.* Philadelphia: Trinity Press International, 1991.

James M. Humber et al., eds.   *Physician-Assisted Death.* Totowa, NJ: Humana Press, 1993.

Derek Humphry   *Dying with Dignity: What You Need to Know About Euthanasia.* New York: St. Martin's Press, 1992.

C. Everett Koop and Timothy Johnson   *Let's Talk: An Honest Conversation on Critical Issues: Abortion, Euthanasia, AIDS, Health Care.* Grand Rapids, MI: Zondervan, 1992.

Barbara J. Logue   *Last Rights: Death Control and the Elderly in America.* New York: Lexington Books, 1993.

Ruth Macklin   *Moral Choices.* New York: Pantheon Books, 1987.

Rita Marker   *Deadly Compassion: The Death of Ann Humphry and the Truth About Euthanasia.* New York: William Morrow, 1993.

Richard C. McMillan, *Euthanasia and the Newborn*. Boston: D. Reidel
H. Tristam Engelhardt Publishing Co., 1987.
Jr., and Stuart F.
Spicker, eds.

Harry R. Moody   *Ethics in an Aging Society*. Baltimore: Johns Hop-
                         kins University Press, 1992.

New York State Task   *When Death Is Sought: Assisted Suicide and Eu-*
Force on Life and   *thanasia in the Medical Context*. New York: New
the Law   York State Task Force on Life and the Law, 1994.

Carl Nimrod and   *Biomedical Ethics and Fetal Therapy*. Waterloo,
Glenn Griener, eds.   Ontario: Wilfrid Laurier University Press, 1988.

Sherwin B. Nuland   *How We Die: Reflections on Life's Final Chapter*.
                         New York: Knopf, 1994.

Russel D. Ogden   *Euthanasia: Assisted Suicide & AIDS*. Montreal:
                         Perreault Goedman, 1994.

Kevin D. O'Rourke   *Medical Ethics: Sources of Catholic Teaching*.
and Philip Boyle   Washington: Georgetown University Press, 1993.

The Park Ridge Center   *Active Euthanasia, Religion, and the Public Debate*.
                         Chicago: Park Ridge Center, 1991.

Timothy E. Quill   *Death and Dignity: Making Choices and Taking
                         Charge*. New York: Norton, 1993.

Thomas Scully and   *Playing God*. New York: Simon and Schuster,
Celia Scully   1987.

Marilynne Seguin   *A Gentle Death*. Toronto: Key Porter Books, 1994.

Earl E. Shelp   *Born to Die: Deciding the Fate of Critically Ill
                         Newborns*. New York: Free Press, 1986.

Richard C. Sparks   *To Treat or Not to Treat: Bioethics and the Handi-
                         capped Newborn*. Mahwah, NJ: Paulist Press,
                         1987.

Robert F. Weir   *Ethical Issues in Death and Dying*. New York:
                         Columbia University Press, 1986.

Mark Wicclair   *Ethics and the Elderly*. New York: Oxford Uni-
                         versity Press, 1993.

Index

can guide euthanasia decisions,
157-63
social self
and autonomy, 35-36
Society for Medicine and Law
(Haifa), 50
Sophocles, 58
Stephany, Theresa M., 111
Stokley, Jennifer, 193
suffering
as a complete evil, 58
suicide
as constitutional right, 92-93
forms of
autoeuthanasia, 18-20
emotional (irrational self-murder), 18
justifiable, 18
frequency in U.S., 81
and legalizing euthanasia
would encourage suicide, 78-83
con, 84-89
would harm society, 64-71
con, 72-77
methods of, 106
prevention of, 80-82, 97
see also autoeuthanasia; physician-
assisted suicide
Suicide (Durkheim), 163
Swomley, John M., 152

Talmud, 39
Taylor, Phyllis, 140
terminal illness
allowing natural death in, 116
defined, 76
termination-of-suffering clinics
(TSCs), 60
termination of treatment, 108-109,
167-69
court cases on

Bouvia, 18, 133
Quinlan, 73-75, 93, 151, 168
and *Roe v. Wade*, 56
euthanasia vs., 22-23, 104
withdrawing vs. withholding
treatment, 151
Theresa, Baby. *See* Pearson, Theresa
Ann Campo
Tong, Rosemarie, 146
treatment, cessation of. *See*
termination of treatment
trisomy (21 and 13)
and euthanasia, 187, 189
Trumbull, Patricia Diane, 25
Twycross, Robert G., 108-109

unconscious, vegetative states
and euthanasia, 29-30, 47
Uniform Determination of Death Act
(UDDA), 184
Union Pacific Railway Co. v. Botsford,
91, 93

vegetative states
and euthanasia, 29-30, 47
Victoria Times-Colonist, 108

Wahls, Steven A., 107
Walzer, Michael, 34-35
Washington state right-to-die
measure, 75, 79-83, 130, 132, 152-53
Whalen v. Roe, 189
What to Expect the First Year
(Eisenberg et al.), 178
whole-brain death, 182
Winslade, William J., 157
women
and euthanasia, 85
World Federation of Right to Die
Societies, 135